O

MW01259871

)••

A Catholic Man's Guide To Breaking Pornography Addiction

Dreck Masters

Contents

A Note From The Author

I'm not a psychologist... or any other kind of doctor. I'm not even a counselor. I'm not a priest or a great theologian. I have no college degree... or even a high school diploma. I'm not a mystic or saint, and I have no claims of the miraculous—other than the common-life miracles that can only be described as miracles because they are so wonderful. I'm just a common man who has a common problem... but who has found a solution. And I want to share it with you.

The solution isn't new. It's not complicated. I'm giving you only what was given to me. The Catholic Church gave it to me, my counselor gave it to me, and other men gave it to me. It's always been available for anyone to discover. I happened to discover it in a unique way and want to share it with you in a unique way.

I hope you'll make the best of all I give in this book... and I hope you'll share it with others.

At the end of this book, I have listed a number of questions to be used as discussion starters in support / accountability groups. You can use these, or order workbooks, also available on Amazon.

Part 1 – You and Pornography

If you have this book, either A – you have a pornography/masturbation addiction and you want help out of the cage you find yourself in or B – someone who cares about you gave you the book because they think you need help.

To those in situation A:

I hope you know what you're in for. This won't be an easy ride. There are no half commitments here. It's all or nothing, because a half-hearted attempt will *not* work. Believe me—like you, I've tried that. It never works.

This book is going to ask some difficult questions, make you think about some uncomfortable things, and draw a hard line in the sand. As you finish the book, you'll have a choice. Do you join the side of purity, or do you sit and rot in the life you've learned to embrace?

But in the midst of the difficult demands that I'll make, I also offer something else—something you might not have known for a long time. Something you might have stopped believing in. I'll offer hope. Hope that you *can* break those chains. Hope that you *will* be able to, once again, be at peace with God, yourself, and your family.

So don't despair... but be advised that the journey you're about to embark on is not for the weak hearted. God meant for men to be strong—in will and in holiness. He'll accept nothing less. But He will also give you the strength to achieve it.

To those in situation B:

Someone thinks you have a problem. The thing you need to do right now is to stop and consider something. If you do not have a problem with pornography, then simply stop looking at it. Right now.

Why? Because it's a mortal sin to look at pornography. It's also a mortal sin to masturbate.

If you try to stop and end up back in the same routine again, then admit to yourself that you are addicted. If you can't do that, then put this book down and store it somewhere until you can be honest with yourself. When that time comes, go back to the above message meant for those in situation A.

Chapter 1 – Axioms

Let's start this journey by establishing what we, as men, can agree on.

Beauty

Axiom #1: Women are beautiful.

More beautiful, in fact, than men are. But there's more to it than beauty and comparison of the sexes. The involvement in beauty is different between men and women.

Men are projectors. We want to create beauty. We write poetry. We write songs. We build things. We paint beauty. We do everything we can to take part in beauty... but it's always an expression with us. We are designers (creators) by nature.

Women, on the other hand, absorb it and become beauty. Men might make wonderful paintings. Women will know where to hang them. Men might design fabulous clothes. Women know how to wear them.

Obviously, this isn't a strict rule. I don't in any way mean to insinuate that a woman cannot create a beautiful design, or that every man can. I'm just trying to point out that men in general want to make beauty—they want to express something that they themselves are not. We might not have called Shakespeare beautiful, but no one can deny that his sonnets are beautiful. In this way, man is like God. God created things (waterfalls, rainbows, trees, animals, etc.) that are beautiful. Even without appreciating the beauty of God, we can appreciate the beauty of his expressions/creations.

But everything a woman does mingles beauty from the outside with the beauty inside herself. She brings the beauty to perfect fulfillment as a part of her own being. She finds a pretty dress, combines it with the shoes she had been saving for a special occasion, and paints her eyes a special shade that will coordinate the clothing. And when she's finished, she looks absolutely stunning. However, the second she steps out of the costume, they become empty shells. Her own self was what made them beautiful, and they are nothing without her body to fill them. In this way, woman is like God. Whereas God Himself is true beauty, and His very nature is the source of His beauty, so a woman is beautiful herself, and continues to be beautiful even when the clothes are absent.

Furthermore, a woman's beauty is not limited to her skin tone or the shape of her face and body. Her beauty resides within her and spills over into everything she does. She kisses a hurt child and makes him feel better. She moves into a house and immediately finds ways to make it a home. She flashes a smile to someone depressed and makes life just a little more bearable. Her very voice sooths the soul.

I cannot stress enough that we recognize this beauty. As we venture into the reasons behind addiction to pornography, the central idea that women are beautiful can never be forgotten.

Women are beautiful. This is by God's design, not by our opinions. He meant for the woman to be beautiful, and He meant for men to behold such beauty in awe and reverence.

Sex

Axiom #2: Sex is good.

It's fun. If it weren't, there'd be no need for this book, because people rarely get addicted to things that aren't fun. The only other point we need to make on the enjoyment of sex is that God *meant* for it to be fun.

But sex does more that provide a thrill. It also produces babies.

There's an argument to be made for babies being a curse rather than a blessing. This book isn't concerned with that argument. The only point I have to make is that babies (no matter how difficult they are) are necessary. Without them, there'd be no next generation.

Fun and procreation are the two natural properties of sex that make it good. But it barely scratches the surface. In sex, we men are able to enter into a supernatural union. It's very clearly defined when Jesus said, *"For this cause shall a man leave father and mother, and shall cleave to his wife, and they two shall be in one flesh."*[1]

So we have two natural qualities of sex (fun and procreation) and one supernatural quality (unity). The natural quality can be present without the sacrament of marriage. The supernatural quality cannot.

But there is a fourth quality I want to address—one that seems to fall between the natural and supernatural. This goes back to the first point I made, about the beauty of the woman. In the act of sex, man does something peculiar—something almost foreign to his nature. Man embraces and becomes beautiful himself. His tendency to create beauty is put on hold, while he, in a fit of passion, becomes one with beauty and enjoys it for its own sake. He and the beautiful woman wrap body, emotion, and soul together, so that man can partake in the beauty he holds in such reverence. He touches the untouchable.

This can also take place outside of marriage... but doesn't come to perfect fulfillment *without* the sacrament.

Axiom #3 – Sex is powerful.

The idea of 'free love' started somewhere in the 60's. There may have been a few out there (probably more women than men) who considered the concept to mean that we all love each other as brothers and sisters... bringing harm to no one, and treating everyone as we would want to be treated. A fair revision of the 'Golden Rule.'

But the vast majority of people understood it to mean 'free sex' and not free love at all. As we all know, free sex means

---

[1] Mt:19:5

the total absence of love. Sex *without* love. Free love actually means freedom *from* love.

It was a social experiment, and it failed miserably. It may have been prompted by the development of drugs which promised to allow women to have sex without becoming pregnant. Or perhaps it was just all the other drugs that passed around through the 60's, warping people's ability to reason... giving them hope that a sin might be committed without consequence. And it's still happening today... even though it's not called 'free love' anymore.

Whatever the reason for the experiment, the real consequences are everywhere we look. Teenage pregnancy, venereal diseases, sexual addiction, sexual abuse, sexual perversion, and finally a complete lack of sexual control.

What people are failing to acknowledge is the power of sex. Notice I didn't say that people fail to *understand* or *see* the power of sex. No one could be that blind—even if they closed their eyes. Sex is probably the most powerful carnal appetite... even more powerful than hunger and thirst. After all, governments rarely make laws concerning how much we can eat and drink (except in very recent times where good health is slowly becoming a new god). But just about every government and religion throughout all history has or had laws concerning sex. And not just institutions, but cultures and social norms as well. Everywhere you look, you will find restrictions on sex. Not because it is bad, but because it is powerful. And, when abused, is dangerous.

St. Thomas Aquinas understood this well. He had committed himself to a life of chastity and abstinence. While on his way to becoming a priest, his brothers abducted him and locked him up, in hopes to change his mind. When all their arguments failed, they sent a woman in to tempt him into impurity. St. Thomas, in a rage, grabbed a burning log from his fireplace and swung it violently at her, chasing her from his room.

He saw that lust would kill his commitment to God. He saw the power of what was before him. He did not try to deal

with the temptation. Instead he chased the temptress away...
and would have fled himself were he not locked up.

St. Thomas, one of the greatest thinkers of the Church,
later wrote the following:

> *"folly, in so far as it is a sin, is caused by the spiritual sense*
> *being dulled, so as to be incapable of judging spiritual*
> *things. Now man's sense is plunged into earthly things*
> *chiefly by lust, which is about the greatest of pleasures;*
> *and these absorb the mind more than any others.*
> *Therefore the folly which is a sin, arises chiefly from lust.[2]"*

The folly he speaks of is the opposition to wisdom that
men experience through sin. He saw that lust could drive reason
away from a man's heart. He saw that it could literally destroy a
man's way of thinking.

Men

Axiom #4 – Men are obsessive

Men are never *mildly interested* in something. Their
interests are usually wholehearted or not at all.

Some men find one thing and stick to it their entire lives.
For example sports, gardening, or video games. Others switch
from one thing to another, changing as often as every few
months.

But they're never half-assed about it. They dive into it,
surround themselves with it, absorb it, and they're (often quite
suddenly) *all about* it. They're usually also ready and eager to
share their obsession with anyone and everyone who will listen.

---

[2] Summa Theologica Q46 A3

Adding Up

Axiom #5 – Axiom 1 + 2 + 3 + 4 = Disaster

When you add all this up, you have a potential for something highly destructive. Every man is tempted by beauty and by the good of sex. When he gives himself completely to it, without constraint, he is suddenly a captive—a slave to something so powerful he forgets how to control it. The power of sex destroys him.

Many men are experiencing this today—more than ever, in fact. Pornography has claimed a throne in our society. It rules its subjects with a heavy whip. It is harsh in battle and even harsher in victory. And men, one after another, are falling to it.

The purpose of this book is to give men the tools necessary to fight back. Or, at least, to tell them where they can find these tools. I hope, in the end, we can take back the throne.

Chapter 2 – Pornography

What is Pornography?

Pornography, defined by the Encarta ® World English Dictionary, includes "films, magazines, writings, photographs, or other materials that are sexually explicit and intended to cause sexual arousal."[3]

Notice that the definition doesn't say that the images must include nudity. After all, many paintings and statues throughout history are of the naked body without being pornographic at all. And many movie scenes are very much pornographic without showing a single nipple or vagina. Black Snake Moan, for example.

Another good definition for pornography comes from the Catholic Catechism: *Pornography consists in removing real or simulated sexual acts from the intimacy of the partners, in order to display them deliberately to third parties.*[4]

I once heard a man say, "I can't tell you specifically what pornography is, but I sure as heck know it when I see it." I think we all do... especially men. More often than not, when men ask, "What is pornography," they want to know when they are sinning and when they are not... or rather, they want to know what's excusable and what is not. The answer, as we'll discuss later, has nothing to do with what pornography is.

Ultimately, the definition of pornography doesn't matter. Not to most men anyway. Certainly not to anyone who needs this book. It might be helpful for someone who is involved in some sort of public rating system. As for us, we're concerned with a much deeper question.

---

[3] Encarta ® World English Dictionary © & (P) 1998-2005 Microsoft Corporation.

[4] Catechism of the Catholic Church, Paragraph 2354

When does it become a sin to look at a woman? Where is the line between *'appreciating the beauty of God's creation'* and *'lusting after another woman'*?

There's plenty of controversy in that area. Especially for the men who want to justify certain behavior. I once talked to a group of men who insisted there was nothing wrong with a topless bar, as long as they didn't try to imagine themselves having sex with the waitresses.

Perhaps for some men, the line might be rather blurry. But for us, for the men who have been literally enslaved by the pornographic industry, the line is very sharp, clear, and easy to see.

The body of any woman other than your wife is off limits.

It doesn't matter whether we're looking at her or just thinking about her. It doesn't matter if she's fully clothed, scantily clad, or completely naked. If our focus is on her body, then we're sinning or putting ourselves in the occasion of sin (which is a sin, in and of itself).

Why Is Pornography Bad?

Most of the time, as I looked at pornography, I had a very real sense of sinning. I knew what I was doing was wrong, knew why it was wrong, and simply hated the fact that I was still doing it. In fact, I hated myself *for* doing it.

But every now and then, especially when I was resisting temptation, a strange thought would come to my head and reside there, nagging me to succumb to its suggestion.

The thought was, "Why are you making such a big deal out of this? You're not harming anyone by looking at these pictures. The women wanted to make them. The publisher wanted to publish them. You want to look at them. Everyone involved is a consenting adult."

That's the devil talking. Deep down, I knew exactly what was wrong with pornography. I knew exactly why taking part in it was sinful. But I wanted to rationalize, because by mind and body had become so much in love with it. I was fighting myself. I wanted the freedom to sin without feeling guilty.

Of course, it didn't work. If I succumbed to the temptation, I entered into a deep state of self-loathing. But for the benefit of those who go through such battles, I wanted to briefly go over some of the evils that are intrinsically part of the entire pornography industry.

The Catholic Catechism gives a summary of the evils caused by pornography in article 2354:

> [5]*Pornography consists in removing real or simulated sexual acts from the intimacy of the partners, in order to display them deliberately to third parties. It offends against chastity because it perverts the conjugal act, the intimate giving of spouses to each other. It does grave injury to the dignity of its participants (actors, vendors, the public), since each one becomes an object of base pleasure and illicit profit for others. It immerses all who are involved in the illusion of a fantasy world. It is a grave offense. Civil authorities should prevent the production and distribution of pornographic materials.*

That one paragraph packs a powerful punch... and *still* doesn't address all of the problems created by pornography. So let's dive into a little more detail.

Pornography and God

Simply put, pornography is bad because God tells us not to do it. It is an offense (a grave offense) against Him. That means viewing pornography is a mortal sin—one that (unless we repent)

---

[5] English translation of the Catechism of the Catholic Church for the United States of America, Copyright © 1994

prevents us from receiving communion and entering into heaven. It cuts us off from sanctifying grace.

Not that we would ever be so bold as to question the will of God, but you might be wondering why He is so solid on this sin—why He would be so rigid.

Let's look at what Jesus says about sex and the bonds of marriage. Specifically, about marriage itself, and the nature of the bond between a man and his wife:

> "And there came to him the Pharisees tempting him, saying: Is it lawful for a man to put away his wife for every cause? Who answering, said to them: Have ye not read, that he who made man from the beginning, made them male and female? And he said: For this cause shall a man leave father and mother, and shall cleave to his wife, and they two shall be in one flesh. Therefore now they are not two, but one flesh. What therefore God hath joined together, let no man put asunder. They say to him: Why then did Moses command to give a bill of divorce, and to put away? He saith to them: Because Moses by reason of the hardness of your heart permitted you to put away your wives: but from the beginning it was not so."[6]

Hmmm... "from the beginning, it was not so." What does that last line mean? God allowed men to sin, even though it was always a sin?

No. That's not what it means.

Remember what sin is. Sin is "any willful thought, word, deed, or omission contrary to the law of God."[7]

There are several different kinds of sin. For example, an abomination is a sin that is directly contrary to the nature of God. An "intrinsic evil." Something where the action itself can never be

---

[6] MT:19:3-8
[7] Baltimore Catechism No.3 – Lesson 6

justified by circumstances. An example of an abomination is lying. Lying can never be justified and it is impossible for God to do it. Impossible for God to permit it.

But God is not a sexual being, so we really couldn't call sexual sin like pornography, divorce and remarriage, or even fornication an abomination. What's more, the law of God permitted divorce and remarriage. So it would not have even been sinful.

What Jesus is talking about is the plans God had for man when He created him. God made them male and female. He meant for the two to join each other and become one flesh. He meant for that bond to last until death. This is how God originally designed us.

That does not mean that God creates each person with a 'soul mate' in mind. It means that we function most efficiently (as individuals, as a family, and as a culture) when man commits to one woman and lives the remainder of his life devoted to that woman.

Because man was so far from God's heart (because he had turned away from God), man wasn't able to live up to his full potential. But Jesus, the new Adam, renews our ability to do this. The forgiveness of sin allows us to enjoy the permanent fellowship that God intended for married couples.

This is what Jesus talks about when He says, "from the beginning, it was not so."

In other words, when we view pornography we not only sin against God, we sin against ourselves. We take the design God had given us and toy with it—as if we might be able to improve it somehow. We destroy what's inside of us, and willfully eliminate our potential to be 'the perfect couple' with our wives. We also chip away at the bond between husband and wife, because we invite an outside party into our bedroom.

Who are we inviting in? A woman? One we don't know or care about? No. Not hardly. When we view pornography, we invite the devil into our bedroom. And believe me, Satan loves it there. When you decide that it's time for him to leave, he won't go quietly. He'll clutch on and dig in, and you'll have to make some huge sacrifices before you can clear evil out of your sex life.

You can start that journey now, or you can wait for Satan to dig in further and become even more entrenched in your marriage.

> Note: Even if you're not yet married, pornography is allowing Satan to get a good foothold—he *will* be there on your wedding night if you don't banish him now! The longer you allow him to stay, the harder it will be to banish him.

Victims of Pornography

Pornography victimizes a lot of people... in many different ways.

- **You:** The number one victim of the pornography industry is you and me... and countless other men who have been ensnared by its seductive allure. You're trapped. You've tried to stop looking and you can't. This alone turns you into a victim. But when we add the fact that viewing pornography is a sin (a mortal sin), we can see that the industry is literally trying to kill your soul. The industry is willing to sell your soul, put you into hell, so that it can extract money from your pocket. This doesn't release you from responsibility—your sins are still *yours*. But it allows us to really consider how much we're being used. Someone else is now in control of our most intimate passion. It ought to infuriate you. Pornography has destroyed jobs, marriages, families, and has brought men to financial, spiritual, and physical ruin. Even if you haven't reached that ultimate low spot yet, even if you're

14

still falling, please wake up and realize what's really at stake.

- **Your Spouse:** When you got married, you took a vow. You promised to give yourself to your wife completely. You promised to keep all sexual relations (in mind, body, and soul) between yourself, her, and God. Every time you view pornography, masturbate, think of pornography, think of other women while having sex, or even look through the lingerie ads to arouse yourself, you violate her rights as a wife. Pornography stole her husband. Don't ever think your spouse is being too rash if she enforces a strict "no porn" rule in her house. She has every right, as she's been personally assaulted by it.

- **Your Children:** Just as you were a target for the industry, so will your children be... if they aren't already. Both men and women alike are being bombarded daily with images. But so are young teenagers (have you seen the commercials during teen-targeted sitcoms?). And even, it's sad to say, very young boys—even as early as 8 & 9 years old. And it's not just that they're being targeted. There's the fact that the time you spend viewing pornography would be much better spent with your family. Like your spouse, your children have had something stolen from them. Their father. Their role model. He now belongs to something else, and believe me—they miss him.

- **Actresses:** The industry goes after girls at a very young age. We won't even touch on the underage illegal industry—just the legal portion of it destroys the lives of hundreds of women every year. An 18 year old girl finds out that she can pay off her shopping debts and get out of the financial bind she's in *just* by taking part in a flick or two. She's young, naive, and still trying to prove to her parents that she can 'make it on her own.' And so she does something that she'll regret for the rest of her life... and something she can *never* erase. Not only will the movie itself (she has no control over where and when the producer sells this movie) follow her for the rest of her life, the sin will also. Her memory of it and her shame will never go away. Sometimes, shame can bring us closer to God. But for some women, for those who can't quite see God's mercy, it pushes them further away from God and brings them to despair. Perhaps even to the point that they get more heavily involved in the industry and never look back to think about the possibility of accepting Christ.

- **The Public:** Have you ever parked in front of a peep show or a porn shop and watched the people going in and out? Are those the kinds of people you would want to have around your family—your kids? A neighborhood is made up of people, including the people who have become a slave to their sexual passions... or sexual perversions, which pornography addiction often leads to. People used to purposely avoid living in neighborhoods that promoted such shops. But now that kind of stuff is in every home in America, being transmitted over a few wires. Easy to get to, easy to hide. Pornography no longer has a 'lair'. It's destroying the public from the home now. Every year, thousands of more men are being sucked in. Men with families, who are, by degrees, losing their manhood.

- **Women in General:** Remember our first axiom? Women are beautiful. They have a *right* to be beautiful. We have a *duty* to view their beauty in awe and reverence. Pornography degrades women. In the minds of men, it turns women into nothing more than sexual toys. A play

16

thing to be used in secret and then cast off. Little by little, as a man becomes more addicted and more oppressed, he loses all respect for women and their beauty. A creation of God—one of his most wonderful gifts—is turned into an object. Women who have respected themselves and God their entire lives are now thought of and treated worse than animals. This is a tragedy—one that can only be fought by completely eliminating pornography from our lives.

- **The Unborn:** Yes, that's right. The unborn. Pornography must have women to film. Women, having sex, become pregnant. Birth control, no matter what kind, does not always work. Eventually, most women in the industry are faced with a decision: kill my child and continue my career, or stop making films. The number of abortions performed directly because of pornography is staggering. Every time you view pornography, you're taking part in that.

Enough victims for you? Can you see clearly now that it doesn't matter if we're talking about consenting adults? Pornography is a killer. It is destructive to everyone, not just those who take part in it. It is never right. It is never permissible. Soft or hard, it is something we must fight against, both in our minds (by not viewing it or thinking about it) and in our lives (by voting against it locally and urging others to avoid it at all costs).

Pornography and Real Sex

As quoted earlier, one of the Catechism's arguments against pornography is that it creates a fantasy world in the mind of those who watch it. A boy who grows up watching pornography comes to think of sex as a self-serving act. The entire thing is there only to please him. He turns it on at will— whenever he's in the mood. And when he's finished with it, he wants to move on immediately. The woman is forgotten, because she was only a part of his imagination to begin with.

In real life, we see that it's much different. Any married man will tell you, a woman doesn't just spread her legs every time her husband wants her to. Sometimes a man will work for days just to seduce his own wife. And often, all that work is still not enough, and his wife has a headache, is menstruating, or just doesn't feel like it.

Also, a woman doesn't disappear from the bedroom after a man has his orgasm. In fact, she continues to try to interact long after he's lost interest in sex. She wants intimacy—real intimacy. Men want to sleep. Women want to 'talk'.

Men who have a selfish understanding of sex aren't prepared for this. They often find themselves annoyed and irritable when they are turned down, and more irritable after sex because they feel as though the intimate moment is over. What they don't realize is that sex is only a small part of intimacy, and that the *before* and *after* matter just as much as the *during*.

Sex is a fantasy in the mind of an addict. When such men are forced to deal with reality, when they have to encounter real life sex in the sacrament of marriage, they fail miserably. Intimacy becomes a myth to them, because they can no longer experience it. They've mangled their perception so much that they miss out on one of the most enjoyable activities God has created.

Note to single men:

Much of this book focuses on married men and married life. This is because *most* men in the world will, sooner or later, be a married man. As a single man, you might be tempted to view your addiction as something temporary. You might think that your compulsion will just 'wither away' when you finally find the right girl and get married.

Nothing can be further from the truth. I myself was addicted long before I met my wife. And while the problem subsided a little during our first few years together, it came back with a fury later on. Every married man will tell you that marriage is NOT the answer to the problem. What's more, marriage, which is much more stressful than single life, will make it even harder to break your addiction. You might not understand right now—mainly because you haven't experienced marriage. But you *must* believe us on this.

If you don't deal with the problem now, before you find your life-partner, it will create huge problems in your marriage. It could end up *destroying* your marriage.

Consider your ideal woman. Do you want to present to her a pure man, who's strong, masculine, and fully capable of leading the family? Or do you want to give her a weakling? A man who can't deal with marriage and will succumb to outside forces, bringing your marriage to its knees?

Follow the instructions in this book and free yourself from the addiction now, before you offer yourself to a woman.

Chapter 3 – Addiction

Addict: One who is given to some habit, especially to the use of narcotic drugs.[8]

I remember once having a conversation with a coworker. The subject: marijuana. He claimed that a certain researcher was once commissioned to do a study on the abuse of weed. His findings were shelved, claimed the coworker, because his conclusion was that marijuana had no physically addicting properties. This, he said, was why marijuana was okay... not dangerous at all. You cannot become physically depended.

I always look back on that conversation, scratching my head. How odd, that someone would claim something was not dangerous because it wasn't physically addicting. After all, gambling is not physically addicting, and yet the habit is so strong that it ruins many people every year. And so is shopping, hoarding, sex, television, virtual games, eating, video games, etc. Even Facebook. In fact, most activities and behaviors can become habit forming. Most can cause real problems in a person's life. Many of them can destroy a person's life. Remember the axiom— sex is powerful, and when misused, dangerous.

I won't argue for or against the use of marijuana... for medical or any other purpose. But to assume that it does no harm just because a person will not go through physical withdrawal when quitting is a grave mistake.

Some people will argue that all the activities mentioned above do, in fact, give people a chemical high. And some will go so far as to say that the chemical itself is what people get addicted to. I think this is kind of over analyzing things. And what's more, this kind of theorizing is not productive.

In our society, we use the word 'addicted' to mean some sort of habit that we are not able to quit on our own. The question is, are you actually 'addicted' to pornography and masturbation, or are you just going through a phase?

---

[8] Funk & Wagnals Standard Desk Dictionary © 1984

When I first began seriously researching how to stop, I found a lot of websites with questionnaires. Surveys that will tell you whether or not you have a real porn addiction. They posed dozens of questions like "Have you ever spent money on pornography?" and "Have you ever deleted your history so that no one would know you were looking at pornography?" Then, at the end, they said that if you answered yes to any of the questions, you might need help.

As a marketing consultant, I recognized the technique. When selling something, you never ask a question unless you already know the answer. They set up the questionnaire so that there would be very few men in the world who could answer "no" to *all* of the questions.

It seemed kind of silly to me. But other men have told me they found it helpful. So here it goes. Here is my questionnaire to find out if you are addicted (in the modern use of the word) to pornography and/or masturbation.

1. Have you tried to stop looking at pornography and/or masturbating and not been able to quit?

If you answered yes to any of the questions above, then you have an addiction. You need help.

The fact is, I think most men know when they have an addiction. And honestly, if they aren't ready to admit to it, then they won't find this book useful anyway. This book is not for the uncommitted or uncertain. It's not for anyone still in denial. So I won't waste any time trying to convince someone they need help.

But at the same time, we need to take a serious look at addiction and understand why a habit binds us so solidly to certain behaviors.

When Is It An Addiction?

There are 3 – 4 different stages of addiction: Experimental, Misuse/Abuse, Addiction/Dependency, and sometimes Escalation. These stages are generally attributed to drug addiction, and not always directly transferable to pornography addiction. But they *usually* apply. Understanding them might help you see why pornography has such a hold on you.

Stage 1 – Experimentation

Most men went through this stage at a very young age. Somewhere between 10 and 13. Some boys go through this because of negligence on the parent's part. Some boys are outright abused (yes—deliberately showing pornography to a young boy is molestation). But for most men, the exposure isn't so dramatic. It might have been a magazine you found in your dad's top drawer, under his socks. Or maybe you found one in the trash and took it home to examine it further. It could even have been a lingerie catalog you took from your mom's stack of magazines. Or the lingerie section of a common JC Penny catalog.

Wherever and however you found it, it did something to you. It held your attention, and you saw something that was pleasing. You might have understood it, you might not have. But you probably didn't understand that to stare and fantasize about it was sinful. Most boys don't.

Often, by the time boys are able to understand the consequences of viewing pornography, it's too late for them to remain pure. Many, as early as 10 years old, have already been so much exposed to it that they feel hopelessly drawn to it.

Also, at this age, is when most boys first experiment with masturbation. Many boys have fallen into the habit of masturbating long before they're told that it's a mortal sin. This is the sad state we find our Catholic society in.

We've pushed the schools to give sex education classes at earlier and earlier ages... but we glossed over some of the really important issues. I find high school graduates (who have attended 12 years of Catholic schooling) who still don't understand the difference between mortal and venial sins. Very few of the ones who *do* understand realize that pornography and masturbation fall under the 'mortal sin' category.

So experimentation happens at a very early age, and boys quickly move into the next stage before they even realize it. They don't see the trap until it's too late. Many are even in the third stage by the time they wake up, and feel completely helpless against these sins.

Stage 2 – Misuse/Abuse

This stage is very different for pornography and masturbation—in comparison to some of the more conventional addictions like drugs and alcohol. It's different because it blends more with the first stage—experimentation.

In fact, experimentation in sexual things generally *is* abuse. Looking at pornography, whether it's the first time you've done it or the thousandth, is abuse of our sexual nature.

But there is a certain innocence in a boy from the first stage who doesn't know any better. And that innocence slowly disappears as three things happen:

1. He gets older and gains understanding of his actions. He might not see it as a mortal sin—or any sin at all really. But he does begin to see that it's something secret. Something that is shameful even.
2. He begins to use pornography and/or masturbation as something more than just a sexual release. He uses it to relieve general stress at the end of each day. Although usually he does not realize he's doing it.
3. He fantasizes about the women, even while he's not looking at pornography. He begins to look forward to being in his room alone so that he can play out those fantasies on himself.

Of course, not all boys fall into this, and some of them don't start it until they are much older.

The older we get, more responsibility is put on us. We have more and more expectations from outsiders. We become less 'winey' about our problems and develop hard shells to keep people from seeing any pain we experience. In short, we become men. We develop a deeper sense of right and wrong. We find ourselves aware of offences against God, even though it doesn't directly harm someone. In a different age, this might have been enough to break men from abusing themselves.

But in the here and now, with the internet, adult channels, and even PG-13 movies selling sex, sex, sex to us at every interval of our lives, this 'coming of age' isn't always enough to drive out the temptation to abuse ourselves sexually. And many men find themselves hooked, with absolutely no idea how to stop themselves. And so they drift gradually into the third stage.

Stage 3 – Addiction/Dependency

There are many lies men tell themselves to help them deny this stage:

- My wife doesn't give it to me often enough—so it's her fault.
- I'm just much more active in this area than most guys... I can't help that. It's who I am.
- It's just a phase. I'll get tired of it eventually and move on to obsess over something else.
- Boys will be boys. We like women and we like to look at them. God made us this way.
- I'm not married yet. As soon as I get married, I'll get sex all the time and I won't need porn.
- I don't know what the big deal is. I appreciate the human body as God made it.
- It's natural—everyone does it.
- Even animals—monkeys specifically—masturbate.

24

- bla, bla, bla.

I won't go through and refute each of these lies, or any of the other ones. As I said, unless you recognize that you have an addiction, and that you need help, then this book won't do you any good. I'm not here to talk you out of denial. I'm here to walk with you to purity.

So what's the difference between being 'over sexed' and addicted to sex (generally including pornography and masturbation, although many men view pornography or 'soft porn' and then take out their 'sexual build up' on their wives).

Let's start with the act of sex itself. God meant for sex to be a way that husband and wife would come closer together. That doesn't always mean that you should feel butterflies in your stomach every time you have sex. In fact, you very rarely will. But an addiction is always self-serving. And it *always* leaves you feeling more empty. More lonely and isolated. More desolate and depressed. And addiction does not bring you closer to your wife.

You might have noticed that the actual activity (the viewing of pornography and subsequent masturbation) seems much less sexual than it once did. In fact, it might have ceased, long ago, to be a sexual activity at all.

This is called **ritualization**. It can occur differently with different men. And once the ritual starts, it can seem almost impossible to stop. It might happen something like this:

You're in line at the grocery store. You look down and notice the woman in front of you. She has wide hips. You don't notice a whole lot else about her—just that she's wearing tight pants, has wide hips, and that you can discern the outline of her underwear.

You're not necessarily undressing her, right there in the store. But you are thinking about wide hips (or some other part of her body). Perhaps you're imagining how other clothing would look on those hips. Perhaps your thinking of the hips of another girl you know. But you know one thing for sure—you know what phrase you're going to type into Google tonight... even every night for the next month.

You might be able to put the wide hips in the back of your mind for a while—until you can have some time alone with the computer. Or you might not be able to—and have to make an extra long trip to the bathroom as soon as you get home. You might even try to fight temptations for the rest of the night, telling yourself to stop thinking about it and begging God to take the thoughts away.

But eventually, you have your alone time. You might be screaming at yourself to stop now, before you get in too deep, but you sit down anyway and begin to type. Maybe you don't search for pornography right away. Maybe you go to a site that you know links to a site that links to a site that links to a site that links to porn. But you also know that the fight was over once your butt hit the computer chair. Because once you sit down while being alone, there's no turning back.

This is a more sexual ritual, and one that is more common with men who are still fresh in their abuse and addiction. But eventually, it might look something like this:

You're wife is nagging you. Not about the clogged drain or the carpet that needs to be replaced. She's nagging about the fact that you don't know where next month's mortgage payment is going to come from. She wants answers—she wants reassurance. You have nothing to give her, because you're pretty worried about it yourself.

Eventually she leaves. You're walking around, wondering how you will pay that stack of bills. But you find yourself in front of the computer because you just don't have an answer.

And once on the computer, you can disappear for a long time. Hours even, because all time stops (all pain stops) while you stare at the pictures and videos.

These are just two scenarios. It might have variations for you, it might be completely different. But it's definitely not what you experienced the first time you looked at pornography or masturbated. It's become something you don't even enjoy anymore. Something you do just to feel normal for a while (or perhaps to forget the fact that you *don't* feel normal *ever*). And when it's over, you feel guilt and despair much worse than you did in the beginning.

If you've gotten to this point, then you need change in your life. You need to rewire yourself. We'll go over how to do this in great detail later in this book. But for now, know that your first plan of action in this battle is to stop the ritual before it starts. That is, to go all the way back to the beginning. Back to the wide hips. Don't look down! That's where the fight starts— by controlling your eyes.

Stage 4 – Escalation

This one is dangerous. Hopefully, you haven't gotten here yet and never will. But many men do. In fact, some men *must* get to this stage before they can admit to themselves that they have a problem.

Escalation might include any or all of the following:

- Having affairs or one-night-stands with women.
- Hiring prostitutes.
- Frequenting strip bars, peep shows, or even porn shops.
- Viewing more intense, or even illegal, pornography— teens, bestiality, sodomy, even child pornography.
- Exposing yourself to others.

- Voyeurism—watching others when they aren't aware, like 'peeping toms'.
- Having homosexual relations.
- And, in worst cases, rape or child molestation.

If you aren't at this point yet, then stop reading and thank God. If you are, then get help now. Don't wait for it to get worse, because yes, it *will* keep getting worse.

This book isn't adequate to help those who find themselves in a sharp escalation... especially in the illegal activities mentioned here. Any man who is faced with this challenge must make more drastic changes in his life than the ones proposed in this book (even though the changes proposed in this book are plenty drastic).

You will need a special kind of help, coming from people who specialize with your problem. This book might help you, but it probably won't cure you.

If you aren't at this level, beware. It might not seem to you that you could ever have a problem with homosexual images or with child pornography. At the same time, there was probably a point at which you never thought you'd be looking at the stuff you're looking at now.

Escalation occurs for two different reasons. The first, quite simply, is the same reason people move on to newer and harder drugs. Someone hooked on Vicodin builds up a resistance to the drug. So they graduate to percocets or to oxycontin. In the same way, our minds build up resistance, and the same types of images no longer excite us the way they used to.

But the second reason we escalate is more spiritual than physical or mental... and it's something not often talked about by doctors, shrinks, or even in 12 step programs.

To get a better view of it, we need to step back and study the kinds of sexual sins—how they relate to us, to God, and to each other.

We had already mentioned that, according to St. Thomas Aquinas, lust can deteriorate our ability to reason. It happens in an immediate sense, when we try to justify our actions. It also happens as a long term sickness might, where we slowly accept more and more unjustifiable behavior, both in ourselves and in others.

But Aquinas also takes a careful look at the *types* of lustful sins. He categorizes them into groups, and explains how each group is a different kind of offence against God.

Premarital sex and extramarital sex are both natural sins— meaning that man is not going against the natural order when he commits them. God made us so that we are aroused by women. While we might be sinning against our wives, ourselves, and God in an affair with another woman, we aren't sinning against nature.

But most of us *have* sinned against nature, and very few of us know it.

St. Thomas Aquinas specifies that every lustful vice is contrary to right reason. But certain kinds of lustful acts are contrary to the natural order of sex. These include: masturbation, beastiality, and homosexuality.

> *Wherever there occurs a special kind of deformity whereby the venereal act is rendered unbecoming, there is a determinate species of lust. This may occur in two ways: First, through being contrary to right reason, and this is common to all lustful vices; secondly, because, in addition, it is contrary to the natural order of the venereal act as becoming to the human race: and this is called "the unnatural vice." This may happen in several ways. First, by procuring pollution, without any copulation, for the sake of venereal pleasure: this pertains to the sin of "uncleanness" which some call "effeminacy." Secondly, by copulation with a thing of undue species, and this is called "bestiality." Thirdly, by copulation with an undue sex, male with male, or female with female, as the Apostle states (Romans 1:27): and this is called the "vice of sodomy." Fourthly, by*

not observing the natural manner of copulation, either as
to undue means, or as to other monstrous and bestial
manners of copulation.[9]

Even though Aquinas doesn't mention it specifically, child molestation would also be included in the list of unnatural vices, as it is certainly not in "the natural manner of copulation" since children have not reached an age of reproductive ability.

From this, you can see that masturbation is classified under the same heading as homosexuality and bestiality. While it's much more common—even more common than extramarital affairs—it still is a different kind of sin than normal fornication.

When you combine that with the fact that lust, in itself, chips away at man's ability to reason, you have a recipe for escalation into some very bizarre and distasteful vices. Where a natural vice (say, looking at a picture of a woman) can lead to more natural vices (like actually having sex with a woman), an unnatural vice (masturbating) can lead to other unnatural vices (having sex with another man).

Furthermore, masturbation is generally a mixture of natural and unnatural vice. Your mind is focused on a woman (natural) while your body is gratifying itself (unnatural). Mixing such sins can produce a multitude of unlikely perversions... which is why so many things that were once considered shameful in society (like homosexuality) are now acceptable.

This is why it's so important for men to find a way out of pornography and masturbation addiction *before* their habits escalate. It's true, some men might not ever escalate. And some may take a long time to do it. But to think to yourself, "I could never do those other things—I just look at regular pornography and sometimes masturbate," is a dangerous line. St. Paul tells us that we should flee the evil of lust—not dance with it and rely on our natures to keep lust from evolving. *"Flee fornication. Every*

---

sin which a man may practice is without the body, but he that commits fornication sins against his own body."[10]

These are the four stages. Each one can lead to the next very quickly, without warning. The flood can come so suddenly that you could drown without ever realizing the water had risen. The more time you waste not fixing the problem, the worse your addiction will get. But I do want to offer a few words of encouragement:

You aren't alone.

You are NOT Alone in This Addiction

One of the reasons addiction is so hard to break is because it is so isolating. After looking at pornography you feel like a freak. You feel detached from the rest of the world, soaking in your own miserable sin. You hate yourself, and sometimes you hate God for making you the way He did.

Realizing that millions of men across the country feel the same way can help.

The self-loathing, the isolation, the depression—they face this too.

There is a way out.

No matter how long you've been addicted, you *can* escape it. It will take commitment and hard work. You will have to sacrifice much. You will not always fly through it with feelings of joy. But you can be victorious over it, and you can once again be at peace with yourself and with God.

Part of this means communicating with other men who are suffering the way you are. Sharing with them the daily struggles and the feelings of hopelessness—along with the victories and the return of hope.

---

[10] 1 Corinthians 6:18

We'll talk about this in more depth later, in the steps to purity. But for now, it should at least give you hope that this is conquerable. After all, if other men have done it, so can you.

Why Sex Addiction Is Different

There was a time when, if you wanted to look at pornography, you had to go somewhere to get it. Many men *did* go to those places, and many of them quickly became addicted to pornography and masturbation. But the number of men who were willing to go that far (to actually visit an adult store) was so few that pornography addiction wasn't quite recognized as a real problem—at least not as a prevailing problem. A few psychiatrists here and there specialized in sexual addiction, but the vast majority of Americans thought it was something only a few perverts experienced and never thought much more about the problem.

The media has changed since then. Most people, even if they don't want to, can see pornographic images on their television just by turning it on. In fact, many men were first drawn into their sexual addictions by watching rated R (or even PG-13) movies... perhaps watching the nude scenes over and over again.

And then the internet came. With no real, working filter— nothing to separate 'good sites' from 'bad sites.' Viewing pornography suddenly became one of the easiest (and most seductive) sins a man could commit. It's there, it's free, and it's easily kept secret. What could be more attractive to our sexual nature?

Aside from the introduction of porn through the internet, our whole society revolves around sex. As a marketing consultant, I remember one of the first things I learned about using images to entice buyers: an attractive female will *always* outsell any other image. In most cases, the sexier she is the better. It doesn't matter if you're selling to men, to boys, or even to other women. Sexy women sell more.

Every advertiser knows this. And since the social norms are being pushed further and further away from a Christian foundation, advertisements themselves are getting downright pornographic.

With all of this going on, it's literally impossible for a man to go through his day without coming across tempting images.

Recovered alcoholics know not to go to bars. They know to stay out of the beer section of the grocery store. They know they can't go to certain parties.

Recovered gambling addicts know they can't walk into a casino, a bingo hall, or a race track.

But for a sex addict, the entire world is a casino. There's no escape from the overpowering allure of sex. In fact, even if a man could block out every tempting image, and never see another woman again, he still carries with him the tons of sexual images he'd already filled his mind with. The images themselves are the temptation. Merely thinking about them is the sin. And the memory can be a powerful temptress.

It takes some hard core self control to deal with this kind of temptation. It also takes the acceptance of occasional failures, but a constantly renewed commitment to sexual purity. But above all, it takes God's help. You *will not* be able to break this habit on your own.

As we will discuss, you have some unique tools to help you. Some of them aren't available to everyone. My advice is to take advantage of them as often as you can.

The Catholic Approach To Addiction

The traditional Catholic approach to any problem is:

1. Go to confession.
2. Accept God's forgiveness.
3. Vow to do better.
4. Attend Mass frequently.

These four things are the backbone of holiness in our world. You, as a Catholic, cannot obtain holiness without them. They work and they are necessary.

But at the same time, Catholic men often fall into the habit of using these tools as a spiritual bandage. We cover up a bad infection, without treating the infection itself. The infection is the damage we do to our brains when we allow ourselves to become addicted to something. When confession and communion are the only things available, then we would have to pray for God's grace and trust in His mercy. But here in America, much more is available to help men out of this pit. God not only invites us to use these tools, but fully expects us to. In other words, it is an obligation.

But where do we find these tools?

The Venerable Matt Talbot, back in the 1800's, developed a system for dealing with alcoholism. One which was very similar to AA's 12 step program. His legacy as the patron saint for alcoholics has been widely celebrated ever since. A similar system is needed for dealing with sexual addiction.

12 Step Programs

Catholic culture is very slow to respond to societal developments, and sex addiction is a development that took the US by storm in a very short period. Our Protestant brothers and sisters, and even the secular world, were quick to develop programs to deal with it.

Catholics who suffered from sex addiction are either forced to deal with it themselves (in which case, the addiction only grows stronger) or seek help from outside the Church (which traditional Catholics are often reluctant to do). But as Saint Thomas Aquinas did, we must be willing to take what others have to offer. As long as it conforms to Church Teaching, we cannot discount what is helping people make peace with God.

Programs like SA (Sexaholics Anonymous) and CR (Celebrate Recovery) have sprung up all over the place. Very few people can honestly say they are not within driving distance of one such program. As a matter of fact, Celebrate Recovery, one of the few truly Christ centered programs for addiction, is now international and is found in many countries throughout the world.

As we will discuss later in this book, a 12 step program will do several things for you. It will connect you with other men who suffer from the same kind of torment. It will show you that you are not alone in battle, and it will increase your morale (as we all know, a soldier's morale plays an important role and has much influence over the outcome of a battle). It will guide you through some of the tough times. It will show you how to repair the damage that your brain has incurred as you slipped into a sexual addiction.

Counseling

In some cases, probably in most cases, a 12 step program isn't quite enough. Most men need some sort of counseling to get through this. The ideal counselor would be a Catholic man. But we're often limited, and cannot pick and choose who we go to. The important thing is to find someone who recognizes that pornography is a sin, even when it is not an addiction. Someone who understands chastity and purity.

Prayer & The Sacraments

The 12 step program along with counseling will strengthen the traditional Catholic tools. But, and I cannot stress this enough, the sacraments are going to be the real source of holiness. You cannot fight this battle without them. Use them as often as you have to. Use them as often as you can.

Aside from these, prayer—daily prayer—is going to be a powerful weapon against the enemy. Every time you looked at pornography or masturbated, you turned *away* from God. There were times you didn't want to. Times you didn't even feel as though you had a choice (this is an illusion, created by Satan, to make you think you're not in control). There were times you may have even prayed for God to stop you as you were in the very act of offending Him.

But now it's time to face God, and refuse to turn from Him ever again. Not the way you did it before. Not with confession as spiritual bandage. This time you're going to ask for healing and strength. And you're going to use the strength he gives you (no matter how small the amount is) to do great things.

You can only do this if you have a habitual daily prayer life... and the Rosary will be your main weapon.

Pornography is an offence against the dignity of women. More so to Mary, blessed among women. The Virgin Mother of God, a symbol of purity, is so deeply disgraced by pornography. And every time you look at it, you disgrace her.

As a result of feeding your sexual desires—feeding it to the point that it is now eating your very soul—you have damaged your understanding of women. You've destroyed your awe and reverence for women. You've warped your perception of their beauty. And so, you have warped your relationship with our Holy Mother.

Over time, you can restore your appreciation for the opposite sex. And you'll do this by asking our Virgin Mother for guidance, assistance, strength, and most of all love.

If you feel no devotion for Mary, then ask her for it. It might not come right away. In fact, it probably won't. Remember, you yourself have dishonored her to the point that you no longer recognize her beauty. But you must continue to say the rosary, meditating as well as you can on the mysteries and persevering in times of spiritual darkness.

Christ came to us through Mary. She is the new Eve. He comes to us through her now.

Aside from the Rosary, each day should begin with the morning offering and end with an act of contrition.

As you persist in prayer, be it the rosary or simple conversation with God as you drive to work, the Devil (as well as your own selfish desires) will work on you. You'll feel as though the prayers aren't working—because you still feel tempted. You might even fall still, and feel like this was just another failed attempt and something else is needed (we'll discuss failure later in the book). Or you might, at one point, feel as though you've got the problem licked, and you no longer need these tools.

DON'T FALL FOR IT. You will need prayer your entire life. You will *never* be able to find peace without it. Don't neglect it. Don't forget it. It is your daily bread. To stop praying and expect success would be as silly as not eating and expect health.

Chapter 4 – Escape

There was a time in my life that I didn't think escape from pornography addiction was possible. A time when all seemed so hopeless. And I read article after article, book after book, that told me just how bad pornography addiction was becoming in our society. Yet few of them offered a solution—and fewer still (in my opinion, none of them) offered a practical way to escape. Something that any man could follow.

Through different sources, I pieced together a solid action plan that worked for me. And I took that plan, and have presented it here, so that it can work for other men as well.

But I don't want to make you think this will be an easy road. As I have said before (and will say again), this road is narrow and difficult—full of every conceivable trap. There are times, as you travel down this road, you will feel as though it's not worth the effort. After all, who are you hurting if you watch a little porn? And even if it does hurt people, the road to purity is just too difficult, and all you get out of it is freedom. Freedom from this one small thing that doesn't really matter anyway.

You'll feel this way probably because you aren't yet aware of how deeply pornography affects you. Especially during the first couple months of withdraw. So now that I've spelled out all the bad things that pornography does, let's look at the other side of the coin. Let's talk about how much you will get out of purity, and how it will change your life forever.

The Side Effects Of Purity

I'm not going to give you a list of statistics. I'm not going to show you the results of controlled studies and experiments. Everything I tell you is anecdotal—either from my own experiences or from the experiences of other men. So I can't prove anything I say here. But I believe it with all my heart... and I think you will to, as you begin to rediscover purity.

No Fear

Just about every recovered porn addict I talk to says that they can never fully express how great it is to live without fear and paranoia. They had spent so much time telling lies, covering their tracks, and leading a double life. And yes, I myself did all of this.

Every time my wife said she wanted to talk about something, my heart would gallop. Had she seen something in the history? Had one of the kids seen something and told her? Maybe a neighbor had come to the door and seen me looking at something through the window. I was always in a state of panic.

Here's how bad it was: I often fall asleep in the middle of our nightly prayers. And sometimes I finish a sentence with some kind of nonsensical piece of my dream—kind of half sleep talking. What if I said something in that state that would give me away? Something like, "Our Father, who art in heaven, I always look at porn." So every night, I would pinch myself (hard enough to draw blood) in order to keep awake, so that I didn't give myself away in my sleep.

I laugh at that now... but sometimes I cry about it as well.

After I had told my wife everything, and had been clean for several months, she found something suspicious on the computer and questioned me about it. I thought it was unfair, because I had worked so hard to stay clean. But at the same time, I knew the suspicions were valid. Either way though, it didn't matter to my conscience. I knew, without any doubt in my mind, that I had not sinned. I had kept to my word. And even if my wife didn't believe me, I knew that as long as I stuck to the truth (which I was doing) I had absolutely nothing to fear. It's not easy to explain, but I can say I don't ever remember feeling that way before. I've *always* had something to hide. Now, I had nothing to hide. Not even in my thoughts.

I was no longer nervous when someone else was on my computer... wondering if I had accidentally left some remnant of dirty pictures in a public folder. I didn't cringe when my boss called me for a meeting... wondering if the company had started using some new kind of monitoring software. I didn't even care if someone was reading over my shoulder. It's a truly liberating feeling.

But it gets better. It did for me anyway.

Since my childhood, I had a fear of being alone in the dark. It's something most men grow out of when they are teens. I didn't. I never knew why, but every time I tried to sleep alone in the dark, my mind was overtaken with an extreme fear. I actually imagined demons, creeping into my bed with me. I couldn't even shut my eyes. I would either turn a light on, or pray the rosary until I fell asleep—which sometimes took hours.

It's not something I ever told people. Not even my wife.

A few months into my recovery from porn addiction, I found myself alone at night. My wife had to stay with one of the kids in the hospital. Through habit, I turned the light off that night and hopped into bed. I lay there about a half hour in the dark, before I suddenly realized—I wasn't afraid anymore. Since then, I haven't had the fear return.

I can't say that this childlike fear was all because of my sins. I can't say that if you have odd phobias, that you'll magically overcome them. I can only tell you about my experience. And I can know, in my heart, that God granted me freedom from this phobia when I accepted freedom from pornography.

Strengthened Relationships

Chances are, you already know that pornography has intruded on your relationships. Not just with your wife, but with your children, your family, and your friends as well. You probably don't yet realize just how much it intruded.

I myself had spent hours and hours searching for pornography on the internet. In my house, the children knew that if I was on the computer, then they shouldn't bother me. Not to ask me a question or anything else. If they so much as approached me, I would yell at them and make them feel like a bother. And they were a bother—because I couldn't feed my addiction while they were in the room.

40

After a few years years, my daughters stopped giving me hugs. When my wife asked them why, they told her because I didn't like hugs. That I would pull away from them when they approached me.

Now I have so much more time on my hands. I can toss football with my sons. I can help my kids with their homework. I can listen to my daughters' stories or read the stories they wrote and give it my full attention. I can bond with them in a way that wasn't possible before. And now, all of them know that they are NOT a bother to me. That I really think of them as blessings in my life. And once again, my daughters give me hugs when I leave for work and when I get home.

My friends also noticed a change in me. Many of them have no idea what was the root of my problems (although, it will be no secret once this book hits the shelves). But they've commented on the fact that I now seem much more relaxed and at peace. This makes me easier to be around. It makes friendship blossom.

But the most notable difference I can see is in the relationship with my wife. We now have no secrets between us. Satan is no longer in our bedroom.

I cherish her love so much more now. No, I don't live with butterflies in my stomach. Yes, we still argue from time to time. But the arguments are less intense. And those butterflies do, occasionally, return. She, knowing this, is now more in love with me.

Renewed Interest In Love-Making

You've spent a lot of time filling your mind with the images of other women. In fact, you've poisoned your mind with them. So much so that your own wife (a real woman, with real flesh and blood, and really in love with you) doesn't excite you nearly as much as she used to.

For some men, this loss of interest in sex with their wives is more announced—to the point that they cannot have sex unless they look at pornography immediately beforehand.

They've adopted (whether they wanted to or not) a new measuring stick for women. Their standards for an acceptable body are unreasonable... especially for a woman who works, cleans the house, has had children and is raising them, and has had to deal with old age WITHOUT plastic surgery. Men stare at the bodies of thousands of women online, and find they are simply not turned on by their wives anymore.

What's more, they often end up using their wives for sexual gratification while thinking of other women. This is dangerous to a man and insulting to a woman. It is a murder tool for any healthy marriage.

But what if you were attracted to your wife again? What if her body, no matter what shape it's in, had the same affect it had when you were first married—or even when you were dating?

As you starve your eyes and mind, this will happen. The imperfections in your wife's body will disappear. Your body will be trained to think of her, and only her, as the only outlet for sex drive. And over time, her very presence will get the gears turning and the motor running.

Closeness To Christ

Leading a double life is difficult in this world... but it's even harder on the spiritual plane. How many times have you prayed for something, but thought, "Why do I approach God for something when I break His commandments daily? Why should he reward such an unfaithful servant?"

Your sinful lifestyle keeps you from knowing Jesus. Keeps you from accepting His mercy. Keeps you from drawing near Him. Even if you know God loves you, you are shutting his love out.

Christ loves you more than anything created. He knows you better than anything created. As your creator, God accepts you with all your flaws and blemishes... as long as you come to him with an open heart, ready to repent of your sins.

Wouldn't it be great to live in that love? To know, without any doubt, that He will never forsake you?

42

It's real. It's possible. God's love is available, and God wants to give it to you so much. You just have to accept it.

Peace With Oneself

Before my recovery, I was the type who sat in church and recited all the responses, but never sang them. Even when the congregation was singing, I would *say* the words. Yes, it was prayer, but it wasn't the uplifting prayer that really brought me closer to Christ. The kind that glorifies His name. For some reason, I found myself singing about a month or two into my recovery. I couldn't hit all the notes. Actually, I have one of the worst singing voices ever. But I sang anyway, regardless of how well I did it.

I think this stems from the fact that I was so disturbed if I didn't do something correctly. Because of my sinfulness, the imperfections I was born with seemed big to me. If I couldn't be the best at something, then I shouldn't try.

I had an easier time being at peace with my flaws once I had dealt with the ones I could control. I found it so comforting to know that I didn't have to be perfect. That God was happy with my efforts, and enjoyed the praise I gave Him even if it didn't sound great to human ears.

This is one of the things you'll experience as you progress in your recovery. You are human. You aren't perfect. You aren't even close to perfect. You make mistakes, sometimes very silly or foolish mistakes. And sometimes, you're so 'untalented' in an area that it's beyond mistake... it's more like an assured failure. But that's okay! You're allowed to make those mistakes and you're allowed to fail. You are the creation of the only Perfect Being, and He takes delight in your deficiencies.

Other Odd Side Effects

I don't know if any of these will apply to anyone else or not. I just know that these things changed for me and I want to share them with you. As you advance in your own recovery, you'll probably experience many things that had always seemed unrelated.

Tickling – When I first got married, my wife and I used to wrestle around... especially at bed time. She would try to tickle me (I was pretty ticklish) and I would try to give her a wet-willie (which she hated). For some reason, as my heart hardened over the years, tickling lost its power over me. I felt nothing when she jabbed her fingers into my side. About five months into my recovery, she poked me in the ribs, and my whole body squirmed out of control. The games were back, and they were more fun than ever. Because now the kids could take part.

Wet Dreams – I used to have some of the worst wet dreams. They were very explicit, and they involved things that I would never in my life do. Things that were so perverse, I don't dare write them down. I would wake up from them sometimes, feeling so disgusting and ashamed, even though I knew they weren't actually sinful. I had been told that wet dreams would be less explicit as I worked toward purity. I didn't believe it at first (and I still don't know if I would call it a general rule) but that's exactly what happened. Little by little, my dreams were less and less explicit. Now, most of them are actually about my wife!

Looks – When my wife and I first bought our first house, a neighbor came to greet us and welcome us to the neighborhood. He lived about 3 houses away from us. Over the years, I saw very little of him, except at a distance. After about 10 years of living there, he visited again. He then commented to one of the other neighbors that I looked very old and very tired. Other people in my life were also making comments that I almost looked as though I was on drugs—aging so quickly. Only several months into my recovery, I started getting the opposite comments. That I looked younger, somehow, and more refreshed.

There's no telling how many ways pornography is making life harder for you. Each man is different. But I can promise you many things in your life are going to change when you've broken the habit and accepted purity as a way of life.

The Stages Of Purity

As I said, this won't be easy. And breaking away from pornography is going to involve some unexpected pleasures as well as discomforts. But some of it *can* be expected. Through talking with other people, as well as keeping track of my own progress, I've discovered that there is a pattern that most men go through while breaking pornography addiction. In fact, this would probably apply to just about any addiction.

Withdraw

The first stage is probably the most difficult. It will last anywhere from 2 weeks to 2 months. During this time, you'll feel very strong temptations to act out. You'll feel depression, and while you're not depressed, you'll feel disassociated from the rest of the world. You'll walk back and forth, not knowing what to do with yourself... trying to find an outlet for the pent up feelings you have—feelings you don't entirely recognize, let along know how to deal with.

In short, you'll be torn in half. A man within a man.

One man is week. He's been starved for a long time. He will have the drive to keep going. He will tell you that it doesn't matter how bad things get—you *can't* go back. You *must* hold on. He will call on God constantly for support and strength. He will accuse you when you fail, and congratulate you when you succeed.

The other man is strong. He's the one you've allowed to become dominant in your life. He's been well fed and well rested. But now that you're trying to subdue him, he'll be like a wild animal wanting out of its cage. He'll tell you that you can't win. He'll make you feel small and insignificant. He'll put thousands of images in your mind, all of them for the sole purpose of making you return to your old master.

The withdraw stage is often harder for other reasons as well. It happens to coincide with the time that many men confess to their wives. In fact, most men cannot even get *to* the withdraw stage until they've told their wives—because telling their wives is the one thing that really pushes them to try harder to stay clean. But that means aside from going through withdraw, you're also trying to sort out a long standing relationship problem. This compounds the effects of withdraw and makes them even harsher.

Some will say this stage is physical as well as mental. After all, looking at pornography and masturbating releases chemicals in the body. You've been using those chemicals to feel good and to escape your problems. So you might actually have physical symptoms of withdraw.

But mostly, this is a mental and spiritual battle. A battle of wills. Are you strong enough or are you not?

Don't be too surprised if you falter a little during this stage. You're just getting up, and now you're staggering toward your goal. You might step out of line here and there. If you do, deal with it quickly and move on. Go to confession, tell God you're sorry, and get back on the horse.

Also during this stage, you won't *feel* progress. You'll go to support group meetings. You'll go to counseling. You'll worship and pray. And you'll wonder the whole time, "What's the purpose of all this stuff? I don't think it's helping me at all. I don't want to do this, and I don't think I need to."

Remember that as you follow the procedures in this book, the specific steps aren't always going to help you with specific stages of your recovery. You won't get a lot of outside help during the withdraw stage. At least, it won't *feel* like help. But withdraw isn't the only stage of recovery. As you make your journey, you'll reach other stages, and during those stages, you'll be glad that you'd stuck with these procedures.

Your biggest trap at this stage is despair. You'll also probably try to find a substitute. Something to take your mind off your pain. Read the corresponding chapters thoroughly and try to get through this without breaking. It will take all of your energy to fight. But don't give up—relief is on the way.

The Honeymoon

When you've made it through the withdraw stage, you're going to enter into a time of joy. You might call this stage a small gift from God—a taste of heaven. It usually lasts 2 - 3 months.

The trees and grass will be greener somehow. The sky will be bluer. The world will look new and innocent. You'll see everything through a fresh, childlike set of eyes.

If you've stuck with your support group, you'll want to share this. Don't hold back. Let your joy overflow. The other men in your group will appreciate it and feed off it.

You'll also discover new and exciting dimensions in your relationship with your wife, children, and other family and friends. Some of them will notice the sudden change in you. Happiness generally spreads, so don't hold back on that either.

But at the same time, you're making changes and not everyone will immediately appreciate them. Those closest to you have gotten used to doing things a certain way, and they won't be as excited as you are when they have to change their routines.

During my captivity, I spent hours on the computer, completely ignoring my wife and kids. They had gotten used to occupying themselves... not always with the best forms of entertainment. Not only that, but they had gotten used to dealing with conflicts by screaming and yelling insults to one another. Now, suddenly, I was becoming a part of their lives again, and I was holding my anger and lowering my voice during conflicts. While they appreciated this, they also resisted the change. They wanted to sink back into their routines. So much so, in fact, that I was often tempted to give up and willingly return to captivity.

The honeymoon stage is the best time to overcome this kind of resistance. You're new and fresh. You'll have more patience now than you'll probably ever have. You must *show* them that the changes you're making are for the better. They must see your happiness, and you must give yourself to them more fully. Help them in any way you can. Take them on enjoyable outings. Give your wife flowers again (or, if you're like I was and couldn't afford it) write her a love letter. Let it be a honeymoon for everyone.

You're also going to continue to go to your support group during this stage. You should be forming strong friendships (alliances) during this stage. You'll need them for the next stage.

The biggest trap during the honeymoon stage is complacency. You think you've made it now. All is well. You don't need the help you'd gotten. You don't even feel tempted much anymore. Read the chapter on complacency in this book, and follow the instructions, whether you think you need it or not. Part of complacency is thinking you're good on your own. Believe me—you're not.

The Test

Let's face it: the honeymoon can't last forever. Eventually, you're going to have to come down from cloud nine. And when you do, you'll crash. Hard.

Several things are happening here. First of all, you're beginning to forget all the terrible pain you went through during your captivity. You still remember it, but you're removed from it now, so it's not as clear to you. Second of all, as the emotional high wears off, you're having to 'rejoin' life, with all its ups and downs, without that cloud-nine state... but yet without the self-medication you had been using for years. And third of all, you're beginning to realize that some of the problems in your life *aren't* disappearing as you had hoped they would.

All of this will produce depression and anxiety. Probably even worse than you had felt it during your withdraw stage. You'll often wonder why you even bothered to clean up in the first place. Your relationship with your wife still isn't perfect, as you had imagined it was during your honeymoon stage. Financial difficulties haven't disappeared. The car is still breaking down. Your job is still pointless, thankless, and boring. Everything still sucks!

On the upside, you're still clean. Which means you're stronger than you were when you started. But that's not really any consolation, because you won't *feel* strong.

Hopefully, you've continued your support group meetings. Now is when you'll need them. You'll need to lean on a few people, asking for their support. No, they can't fight *for* you. They probably won't be able to give you anything in the way of tangible help. But they can lend their ears, and they can let you know you're not alone in your battle. They'll serve as a refueling point... if only so that you can make it to the next day without your motor dying.

You should have also formed certain habits concerning your wife and kids during your honeymoon stage. Continue with these, even when you don't feel like it. Kiss your wife goodbye when you go to work each morning and hello when you return from work each night. Continue to compliment her, and act as if you really cherish her. Spend time with your kids, even if they're making it harder on you.

Above all, continue to pray. Every day, all day. Let your entire existence be a prayer to God. Thank Him for your purity. Ask for His help as you strive to maintain it. And put your trust in Him.

As with withdraw, the biggest trap here is despair. You'll also begin rationalizing and/or looking for a substitute for pornography.

Maintenance

Little by little, you'll climb out of that depressing testing stage. The transition won't happen all at once, as it did with the previous stages. But you'll find yourself on a little bit of a roller coaster. Somewhat happy for a while, somewhat sad for a while. And maybe some of those humps and dips are very steep and very deep. Guess what... that's what we call life. Normal life. You're there now. You've made it.

You still have plenty of problems. You're not completely happy with the way things turned out. But now you've gained strength, and you can begin to unbend all the kinks in your life.

At this stage, you will need long-term perseverance. Maintain all the practices that helped you through the other stages. Keep a journal, so that you can catch yourself if you begin to fall again. Stay with your support group, not just so you have help, but so you can give back to others what God gave to you.

The big trap in this stage, the one you'll now have to deal with for the rest of your life, is complacency. No matter how long you've been clean, it would only take a few seconds for you to fall again. So be on guard constantly. Shield yourself from temptation. Don't ever think, not for one second, that you are above sin. You are human, and only with God's grace can you stay clean.

Part 2 – The Steps to Breaking Porn

Every successful program for quitting an addiction follows the same pattern.

- You recognize and admit to the problem.
- You admit that you cannot fix it yourself.
- You decide to change and accept help.
- You confess your sin.
- You fix what you've broken (in yourself and in other people).
- You forgive people (and yourself).
- You change your routines and habits.
- You pray for help.
- You help others.

This book will follow a similar outline. What we've added to the normal '12-step' approach is the use of the sacraments and a commitment to purity. Not just kicking the pornography habit, but staying completely clean and chaste.

Now it's time to start taking those steps.

Chapter 5 – Recognition / Admission

The first step to conquering any addiction is recognizing and admitting to the problem. "Oh, that's easy," you say. "I look at too much pornography." Yes, it might sound that easy... much like an alcoholic might easily recognize that the problem as "drinking too much."

But in admitting the problem, we also have to recognize and admit to the solution. For the alcoholic, we would know that a solution like temperance is a *false* solution—it's no solution at all really. Because part of being an alcoholic means that temperance has become impossible. An alcoholic, in order to recover must stop drinking completely—and then must make lifestyle changes that will keep him or her from being tempted again.

But how can a porn addict do this? How can a porn addict say 'no more porn?' It's different than with alcohol, because no one can force an alcoholic to drink. An alcoholic generally won't 'accidentally' take a quick whiskey shot. But a porn addict can very easily accidentally see a photo or video with nudity. In fact, he almost definitely will see it. And once that image is burned into his brain, he will carry it around with him forever—always being tempted to think about it and masturbate to it.

The solution is purity. You can't just stop looking at pornography. You *must* stop looking and thinking about the bodies of other women. Your wife is the only one you can see.

Does that sound scary? Too difficult?

Well, it can be difficult, but it shouldn't scare you. It *is* doable. And I'm going to show you how in the next several chapters.

Impurity Is a Choice

St. Paul lists impurity as one of the grave sins—those which would keep us from going to heaven.[11] If it's a "sin," that means it's a "choice." Whether we're thinking about women or looking at them, no one can *make* us do it. We must *choose* to do it.

The Choice Is Yours

Yes, images can pop in our heads. Yes, our eyes can be suddenly shifted toward a woman who is attractive or not dressed appropriately. And yes, we can get erections from these things. But once we accept it or encourage it, we cross the line from temptation to sin. When we stop trying to push the images out of our minds, when we take a second glance at a woman or continue to gaze at her, or when we touch ourselves, we *choose* to be impure.

Of course, as you will see, there are many things throughout each day that will tempt us to make the impure choice. In fact, even Satan can have free run of our imagination. St. Thomas Aquinas says that the devil can produce images in our minds: *"Both a good and a bad angels by their own natural power can move the human imagination."*[12]

That doesn't necessarily *force* us to think about it. It just presents us with an internal image—one that can be very seductive.

As you try to commit to purity in your life, you'll find these images coming to mind often. They're not all necessarily coming from a demon. Perhaps none of them are. After all, you've filled your head with these images for a long time, and it will take a long time to get rid of them all... or at least to bury them enough so that they aren't constant sources of temptation.

---

[11] Gal. 5:19-21
[12] Summa Theologica Q111 A3 – The Action Of Angels On Men

But we do know that Satan *can* and *does* tempt us this way. And the more committed you are to purity, the harder he will work to change your mind. He will persist, persist, persist. You must resist, resist, resist.

But despite his constant temptations (and those created by your own mind) never forget—the choice to be impure is *yours*. Not *his*. If you fall, it will be your doing. Not his.

Do Not Shift the Blame

While we can't blame our impure choices on the devil, neither can we blame them on others.

One of the common tendencies of an addict is to blame their problems on others, leaving themselves open to continued failure. It's no different for sex addicts.

"My wife doesn't give me enough," is one of the most common excuses. Don't do this to yourself. Realize that God is not going to command us not to do something we don't have the power to do.

Remember in Matthew 19, when Jesus explained the laws concerning divorce? He said that God permitted something because of the hardness of man's heart. In other words, even though God desired for man to be faithful to one woman, he allowed him to divorce and remarry because he knew man was not yet capable of faithfulness.

We aren't living in that age. Jesus has come. He died and rose so that we could fight temptation and sin. He conquered the hardness of our hearts. Therefore, it is now possible for us to be faithful to our spouse and to God.

Man can live without sex. It's true that he does go through periods where the temptation is stronger. Our bodies manufacture semen and sperm, and there is a filling point—a time when the body can produce no more until it gets rid of what it's already made. But we don't need to have sex. God created a very simple way for our bodies to expel it: wet dreams.

Man, as an individual, simply does not need sex. So don't allow yourself to pass off the blame. If you choose to look at pornography or masturbate, then the sin is yours and yours alone. If you have a wife who is refusing you for extended periods of time, then she may well be sinning. But that doesn't excuse any type of behavior from you.

Purity Is Also a Choice

If you've been enslaved for a long time, you may not realize that purity is still a choice. You may have tried it at one time (perhaps many, many times) and failed. And now you've conditioned yourself into thinking that the choice is no longer there. You might think that you *have* to remain impure.

That's another lie that Satan uses against us. You will always have a choice.

But at the same time, the deeper you sink into your addiction, the less likely you are to recognize that choice. So don't allow yourself the luxury of time. Sure, you might be able to put off your conversion for another day, another month, another year. The question you want to ask yourself is how much will you deteriorate during that time.

Remember that lust can create flaws in man's reason. If you continue down the path you're on, can you know for certain that you'll even *want* to change your ways a year from now? And what about the damage (to yourself and to your relationships) your addiction causes during that time? How many people will you hurt? Go back and read about the many victims of pornography. Do you want to be associated with all of that destruction?

Also, don't forget about the escalation that is deeply inherent with the sin of lust. You might not think you could do anything to harm another human being. You might think to yourself, "That's where I draw the line." But hasn't that line been shifting, further and further from purity, ever since you looked at your first picture? If you can't stop looking at pornography, what makes you think you'll be able to stop yourself from molesting a child? What if the temptation were just as strong?

I bring these things up so that you can recognize urgency of your recovery. Yes, you can still decide to fight later, but isn't *now* the best time?

Make the choice. That's all you need. The choice to stay clean.

God's Grace Will Help

You've probably tried many times to quit already. So you're wondering why making the choice now, as you read this book, would be any different. First of all, because you're going to do all of the other steps in this book, one by one, and slowly dig yourself out of the hole you're in.

Second of all, because you're going to ask God for the grace you need to fight.

Yes, you've asked for it before. You've even begged for it. You've cried and pleaded with God to take the temptations away. And you still keep coming back to the same routines.

You have to do it again. Again and again. God will help you as long as you have hope. It might not be on *your* schedule. You don't know when and how He will help you. But God will grant you the grace you need as long as you keep asking for it.

If you feel as though you can no longer pray for God's help (yes, most men who suffer from porn addiction have felt this way at times) then pray that God will make you *want* to pray for help. If you feel no hope, and can't pray for hope, then ask God to help you pray for hope. Come to God in whichever state you're in and allow him to draw you closer to His love.

Remember the prodigal son? He decided to return to his father. But when the father saw him in the distance, the father ran to meet him. The son didn't even have to make the whole journey. In the same way, as long as you are facing God, then God will find a way to bring you to Himself.

But always remember that God's grace is a gift—it's not a right or entitlement. God does not owe us anything. If you don't think you have the grace to do something, then ask for the grace and then try your hardest. If you make it through, and find that you did indeed have the grace, then thank God with your whole heart, and ask for His continued assistance.

God Will Not Do The Work

Of course praying for help is a far cry from expecting God to just lift the temptation from our shoulders. God will not do the work for us. If God kept us from being tempted, then how could we become strong? You wouldn't want a personal trainer to lift weights for you and walk your tread mill, would you? That would be pointless.

God desires you to build strength—to become a powerful soldier in the war against evil. You will accomplish this through hard work, resisting temptation, receiving the sacraments, and praying daily. No one can do it for you.

You'll find help along the way. Even Jesus, as he carried his cross, received help. But that cross was His. It was His hands and feet that were nailed to it. Your cross will be yours to carry. Get help when and where you can, but don't expect the cross to disappear—*ever*. You'll have it for the rest of your life.

You Must Commit

Realizing that you'll have to bear this cross for the rest of your life, you might be tempted to give up. Especially as you face the next few days, and see just how heavy this cross can get.

The commitment you need is a long term one. One that will last through victory, through hardship, and even through failure. Yes, there might be times that you fall. Sometimes you'll just stumble, sometimes you might land flat on your face. But you must commit to getting up again... *every time you fall!*

There must be no question in your mind. You can never allow yourself to second-guess. Every time you think to yourself, "Maybe I can't do it," you must stop your thoughts entirely and forge ahead without thinking at all. To continue such a conversation in your mind, you are giving audience to Satan. Because he will tell you that you can't do it and you must not listen to him. Don't even allow him the time to say it. Don't converse with him. End the conversation with, "I'll do it anyway!" and move on immediately.

That's important—to move on immediately. If you need confession, then save your examination of conscience for the end of the day when you make your act of contrition, and again for when you are in the church, before the Holy Eucharist. To dwell on your sins before that will cause depression and despair. It will give Satan a foothold, so that he can continue with the conversation.

Purity Is The Only Way Out

You started with the notion (you picked up this book with the notion) that you wanted to stop looking at pornography. That is your goal. But before you can step into a porn-free world, you have to understand that porn-free is not enough. In fact, if you try to only eliminate the porn, you *will not* succeed.

Breaking from porn means breaking from anything that tempts you sexually. It means not watching R-rated films with sex scenes—or even avoiding any television that has sensual imagery. It means not glancing through the bra section of a catalog. It means not glancing at the breasts of the girl serving your lunch at a restaurant. It means not staring at a girl's behind while you're in line to pay for groceries.

No Half Hearted Attempts

All of these are things that tempt you. You probably no longer recognize them as temptations because of the ritualization and escalation of your addiction. You might think that a simple outline of a woman, since it doesn't cause an erection or excite you, is 'no big deal.'

This is one of the reasons pornography addiction is so difficult to break. Because of that exact lie. The body of a woman, when you look at it and allow yourself to think about it, creates a small snowball. Once the snowball gets rolling, it's going to pick up more volume. Eventually, it will be too big for you to stop. If you get in the way, you'll just be crushed under its weight. And you'll end up in front of the computer again, looking at all the things you swore you'd never look at.

The easiest way to deal with the snowball (the *only* way to deal with the snowball) is to keep it from ever forming. Stop feeding your eyes. Stop thinking about women. Strive for absolute purity of heart and mind. Your attempt to quit looking at pornography must be an attempt to close your mind off to *every* kind of lustful temptation—no matter how big or how small.

Completely Pure or Completely Lost

Of course, none of us can be completely pure. We are, after all, human. We're subject to bodily weakness as well as spiritual weakness. On one hand, you can be wrong in assuming you only have to stop looking at naked women, and that you'll find your way to freedom without giving up everything. On the other hand, you could easily fall into a trap of, "Oh well—it didn't work. I'm not completely pure because I stared at the jogger in the park. I might as well give up."

Complete purity is the goal. The objective. That's what we're shooting for. An incident (or even a thousand incidents) shouldn't make you feel as though all is hopeless.

At the same time, if you're not aiming for absolute purity, then you are completely lost. You'll sink back into the sin again, and you have no idea to what level the addiction will escalate.

Be safe—make the commitment to be completely pure. If you fall, get back up again and reassert yourself. This is possible with the help of God, and your commitment to purity (recognizing that you're helpless on your own) is the first step.

Now for a recap, which we'll do at the end of each chapter. These are things you should be doing EACH day. Things that you must also keep in mind throughout the day. Before continuing to the next chapter, take a few moments to memorize the list. By the end of this book, you will have memorized what is needed for your transformation.

1. You are recognizing and admitting to the wrongs you commit... as soon as you realize it.
2. You are praying every day.

Chapter 6 – Shine The Light

Over and over again, throughout the Bible, God calls Himself the light. God drives out the darkness in our lives. His truth is blinding, and it illuminates all of our sins. In order to for you to break your pornography addiction, you must allow this to happen.

Light Drives Out Darkness

Let's say your wife is sitting next to you while you work on the computer. She can see all that you're doing. She might even be reading over your shoulder. Would you look at pornography at that time? What about your kids. What if they were watching? Or the neighbors? Your parish priest?

You might find exceptions here and there, but I think it's safe to say that pornography is a deep, dark secret. A few of the boys might joke about it now and then, openly admitting to seeing it, but very few of them want to confess to being an addict. None of them will want to say, "Yeah—I wasted over three hours looking at porn yesterday while I was supposed to be working." Certainly none of them would look at it while everyone is watching. Even while a few people are watching. They (and you) do it alone.

That's why the problem festers—because it is practiced alone and not spoken of afterwards. The more light you shine on the problem (the more people you talk to about it—observing some of the boundaries outlined below) the better chance you'll have of conquering your habit.

Addictions Grow In Darkness

"The eye of the adulterer observeth darkness, saying: No eye shall see me: and he will cover his face."[13]

When we hide what we do, we give Satan a special little workshop—one where he can inflict his own will on us without hindrance. You see, shame is a hindrance to sin. Without shame—without the public feeling of guilt—we might soon be convinced to do all kinds of atrocities. The escalation of your addiction will occur much more rapidly and intensely if you do not find a way to chase it out of darkness.

Think of a wild animal that has been tamed. He will eat from your hands. He will allow gentle caresses, even from children. He will play with a human. But leave that animal alone in the wild, without a taming whip to subdue its instinct, and it will quickly become the same animal it was before. When you try to capture and play with that animal, it will bite you.

The darkness or secrecy of your addiction is the wild. The scrutiny of others is the taming whip. If your sexuality doesn't feel the lashes when it gets out of line, if the shame and discomfort of admitting your sins isn't a reprimand for you, then how can your addiction do anything but grow wild and unpredictable?

Sin Withers In The Light

But when the light shines (when you know that your sins will be open to other people) then your shame will subdue your lust.

---

[13] Job:24:15

"If the morning suddenly appear, it is to them the shadow of death..."[14]

It is for this reason that you must confess your sins. It is for this reason that you must find accountability partners who know your weakness and will call you on the carpet. And it is for this reason that *very* few men are able to conquer pornography addiction until they come clean with their wives.

That sounds chilling, I know. And I would not tell you to go straight to your wife right now and plant this bomb on her. I will discuss it more later. For now, just be aware that for most men, their biggest supporter in the battle against pornography, is the one they've hidden it from the most—as well as the one person it will be most difficult to tell.

Note:

Please read this entire section carefully before deciding who to tell and who not to tell about your habits. There are many occasions where it would be inappropriate to share your struggles with someone. In some cases, it might even be considered sinful. Your actions should always make you blush with shame, and that is the point of telling someone. If you are too open about your problem, it could be that you've defeated the purpose of 'shining the light.'

Using Confession

As discussed in several other places in this book, viewing pornography and masturbation are both mortal sins. That means:

1. You cut yourself off from God, losing His sanctifying grace.

---

[14] Job:24:17

2. You cannot go to communion until you've received the sacrament of reconciliation.
3. You stand in danger of eternal damnation.

These aren't my opinions. They aren't the pope's opinions. They are official teachings of the Catholic Church—actual divine revelations meant to help us get to heaven. What it all means is that you have to go to confession, to a priest, and receive absolution. If you haven't been to confession for some time, then take a good 24 hours to closely examine your conscience and perhaps even make a list of the sins you've committed since your last confession.

Don't be afraid of it. The priest isn't going to chase you out of the confessional. He's not going to yell at you. He's not going to remind you of how bad all these things are. He is, more than likely, going to rejoice that you've been gone so long and have returned to God's rich garden of grace.

Below is a list of several more things that you might not have known about the confessional—things that, when misunderstood, can keep someone from the sacrament. Some of them I myself have worried about during the ten long years I went without confession. Some I have heard from other men who worried about their serious sins. If there's something you're worried about that isn't addressed below, a quick online search can probably answer your question.

- **The priest cannot tell your wife, or anyone else, about your problem.** The priest is under a vow of silence in this regard. He can never give away someone's sins. Even if he were ordered to by law and thrown into prison. No matter how bad your sins are. No matter how important he might think it is that you tell someone else. What happens in the confessional stays in the confessional.
- **The priest cannot make the condition that *you* tell your wife, or any other person, about what you've done.** He

cannot say, "I will only forgive you if you turn yourself in." That would break the vow of secrecy he is under, just the same as if he told your wife himself.

- **You don't have to 'quit' *before* going to confession.** Not in a sense that you have to have a number of clean years, anyway. By going to confession, you are promising not to commit the sin again. That doesn't mean you'll succeed. It doesn't mean you even *think* you can succeed. It just means that you really intend to never commit the sin again. You might have just committed the sin that day... and you know, because of your history, that you'll probably commit it again tomorrow. But as long as you fully intend *not* to commit it, then you can be forgiven. Just as you don't have to clean up before taking a shower—taking a show *is* cleaning up.

- **The priest is human as well, and aside from struggling with the same types of weaknesses, has also heard the same sins from many, many men.** Perhaps you've slipped further down the trail of evil than you want to tell. Perhaps the pictures you looked at were of younger girls than is considered 'normal pornography.' Chances are, the priest has heard the same sins you confess many times. You cannot let fear keep you from healing, and confession is the first dose of medicine. Without it, no other healing can occur.

If you still have misgivings about going to confession, consider this: you don't necessarily have to go to your local parish priest. Not that I advise any man to go confessor hopping (which is a common practice among men with addictions), but for that first time, there's nothing wrong with a little anonymity. Realizing that you'll *never* have to see or talk to this priest again can help you get over that initial fear.

Confession As A Tool

Confession, especially as a scheduled habit, will play a big part in your recovery. You should plan to go to confession at least once a month. Twice a month would be more helpful, especially during your first year of recovery. And of course, you'll need to go every time you look at pornography or masturbate. That might be every week for a while, depending on how well you work your way through this book.

Confession, aside from absolving you from your sins, is a great tool. In most 12-step programs, they advise you to make a routine inventory of your life. Once daily, so that you can see where you've gone wrong and learn from it, always vowing to do better from now on; and once every couple of months so that you can see how far you've advanced (or reverted) in your recovery.

Your daily inventory is your act of contrition each night. It shouldn't take too long, and you don't want to be too scrupulous over small matters. But you do want to take note of your sins, say you're sorry to God, ask for forgiveness, and vow to do better.

Your monthly inventory happens in the confessional or as you examine your conscience just before confession. Again, this will help you see how far along you are in your recovery. Are you still peeking at inappropriate pictures every now and then? Are you paying better attention to your own wife? Are you allowing yourself to be annoyed when you don't get your sexual fix?

But you'll do more than take inventory. You'll say these things out loud. This makes the sin more real, and this is especially important for a pornography addict. You've spent much of your life escaping reality. After all, fantasy is what it was all about from the beginning. It's time to face reality, head on.

The big sins in your life are very apparent to you right now. Perhaps some of the smaller ones are easy for you to see as well. But you'll find that going to confession will sharpen your senses even more.

There was a time when I didn't know or care how long the grass in my front lawn got. It didn't matter to me that it was full of dandelions, crab grass, and many other weeds. It was green—

to me that was a lawn, and that meant I must mow it every now and then to avoid city fines.

But one day I noticed how nice it felt to walk through my neighbor's lawn... and how much it contrasted with my own lawn.

I set out on a mission to clean my yard up. I started by keeping my lawn at the perfect height—literally mowing it twice a week during the heavy spring. Eventually, I realized that I needed more actual grass and less weeds. I seeded, fertilized, and a whole lot of other things. I can tell you, it took me a long time to finally make the lawn look even half-cared for. But by then, I wasn't happy with half-cared for.

I had begun to notice everything about it. Every defect (even the ones no one would ever notice) seemed very large to me. I wanted all the parts of my lawn to be the *same kind* of grass. I wanted it to match. I wanted it to grow at the same rate, which meant watering and/or fertilizing the shaded areas more than the sun soaked areas. I even went so far as to cut down the maple tree in my front yard.

You see—the more I worked on it, the more I noticed. In the same way, the more you go to confession, the more you'll start to see the defects in your soul. Right now it's just pornography. But soon you'll see behavior patterns of selfishness. You'll see laziness and gluttony. You'll see pride. You'll see more and more that you can correct.

This isn't meant to discourage you. It's called growth, and it isn't difficult when taking the proper size steps. For now, what you need to work on are the mortal sins, and the venial ones that normally lead you to mortal sin. Mainly, lust.

This is how confession is used as a tool in your recovery. But it's more than just a tool... it's a sacrament too, and that's what you can never lose sight of.

Confession As A Sacrament

As mentioned before, you absolutely need to go to confession in order to fight this battle. When you go to confession and rid yourself of the guilt of mortal sin, you once again become a child of God.

According to The Catholic Catechism, the spiritual effects of the sacrament of Penance (Confession, Reconciliation, or whatever—different generations called it different things, but the substance never changed) are:

- *reconciliation with God by which the penitent recovers grace;*
- *reconciliation with the Church;*
- *remission of the eternal punishment incurred by mortal sins;*
- *remission, at least in part, of temporal punishments resulting from sin;*
- *peace and serenity of conscience, and spiritual consolation;*
- ***an increase of spiritual strength for the Christian battle.***[15]

That's a pretty serious list there. To tell you the truth, all of them are necessary for your battle against temptation. But that last one, the "strength for the Christian battle" is one that should really speak volumes to you.

But our Protestant brothers and sisters don't have this sacrament. So why are they able to fight off this temptation without it? Shouldn't we be able to also?

Well I can't speak for God. I just know that we, as Catholics, have a special peek into the fullness of faith—one our Protestant brothers and sisters don't enjoy. I can only assume that God will expect me to make good use of what I have. When a Protestant man has a limited view—a limited understanding—of the sacraments and that man does as well as he can, with whatever he has, then I can only imagine that God will bless him with appropriate strength. In fact, I know that God does—because I've seen Protestants do amazing things and bear more

---

[15] Catechism Of The Catholic Church: Article 1496

fruit than I could ever hope to bear myself. Because of their sincerity and unshakeable faith, God works through them. As for me, I have more at my disposal. So I know in my heart that God expects more from me. Since you are reading this book, I can only assume that you are Catholic too. And so I will assume that God expects more from you.

I should also mention here that most Protestant denominations do believe in some sort of confession. They don't understand it as a sacrament, and most don't believe that the priest (or preacher or elder or deacon or whatever word they use for the ministers of their church) has the power to absolve sins. But they do believe in (and encourage) their members to make confessions and openly repent of their sins.

Now in this sacrament, aside from receiving the gifts listed above, you'll also be getting advice from someone who can help you through recovery. You might be lucky enough to find a priest who will agree to be your spiritual advisor. Someone who can monitor your weekly or monthly progress. We'll talk more about that soon. But even if you don't have a spiritual advisor—even if you still go to confession anonymously—you can still benefit from his advice.

There are arguments over just how much our modern priests know about holiness... about just how much they know about God and the Church. Perhaps you're a scholar (a traditional one) and you feel your knowledge exceeds that of your priest.

Or perhaps you don't trust your parish priest. Perhaps under public scrutiny, he has fallen short as a man of the cloth. Yes, the scandals are scary. They really are making it hard for some of us to continue in our faith. You might think to yourself that (even with this terrible addiction) you're a step ahead of your parish priest in the way of holiness.

It doesn't matter. Because there's one thing you haven't done, and that's sit on the other side of that screen. You haven't heard hours and hours of confession, and seen all of the destruction that sin can cause in a person's life. No matter how much a priest knows about God and holiness, I can guarantee you that he's an expert on sin—and *that's* what you need guidance on. On how to avoid this sin.

Aside from that, the priest is also guided, in a special way, by the Holy Spirit. Even if he's in a state of serious sin himself. We are guaranteed by the Church that the priest, despite his standing with God as a man, is still there to speak on behalf of Christ. Concerning Holy Orders, the Catechism states:

> *This sacrament configures the recipient to Christ by a special grace of the Holy Spirit, so that he may serve as Christ's instrument for his Church. By ordination one is enabled to act as a representative of Christ, Head of the Church, in his triple office of priest, prophet, and king.*
>
> *As in the case of Baptism and Confirmation this share in Christ's office is granted once for all. The sacrament of Holy Orders, like the other two, confers an indelible spiritual character and cannot be repeated or conferred temporarily.*
>
> *It is true that someone validly ordained can, for grave reasons, be discharged from the obligations and functions linked to ordination, or can be forbidden to exercise them; but he cannot become a layman again in the strict sense, because the character imprinted by ordination is forever. The vocation and mission received on the day of his ordination mark him permanently.[16]*

Furthermore, St. Thomas Aquinas states, "For all that a man may return to the laity, the character (that conferred to him by the Sacrament of Holy Orders) always remains in him.[17]

---

[16] Catechism Of The Catholic Church: Article 1581 - 1583
[17] Summa Theologica Q35 – A2 – Of the Effect Of Holy Orders

Despite all the rejections that have come up in the past and present propaganda against Catholic Dogma and general Catholic culture, confession with a priest is by far the best way for you to receive the spiritual help you need. That's not to say you can go to confession, and then you'll be healed of this addiction. An addiction is a mental disorder, and will require some mental help.

Finding Accountability

Now aside from confession, you need someone who will hold you accountable in your weekly, or even daily, struggles. This isn't necessarily going to be a mentor, or someone who will guide you. This is going to be someone you will report to on a scheduled basis. Someone who might get reports from the adult filters you install on your computer (we'll talk about that soon).

There are varying opinions on who this person (or persons) should be. Some will swear that their wives are in the best position. (If your wife still doesn't know about your addiction, don't worry—we'll discuss that in this chapter also.) Others argue that it puts a spouse in a policing role, which very rarely works. It might also put a burden on your wife that she does not want. But ultimately, it's something you and your wife will have to discuss openly and honestly... and it probably won't be a comfortable discussion for either of you.

Most men agree that another man is the best accountability partner. I would advise that you have several partners. At least one of them should be familiar with the recovery process, and should be further along in the process than you are.

An accountability partner will do two things:

1. He will be there for you when you need to reach out and talk to someone about your temptations and triggers (we'll go over this in more detail in Chapter 9).

2. He will call on you occasionally and ask you specific
    questions regarding your recovery: How long has it been
    since you last sinned? How well are you standing up to the
    temptations? What are you doing to fight the urges? How
    are you changing your approach if it's not working?

What an accountability partner does *not* do is condemn
you. The shame that you feel when giving a 'bad' report is
natural, and he knows it. He isn't there to make you feel worse.
He is only there for you to lean on, to help you, and to make sure
you're not avoiding the reality of your sins.

An accountability partner is all about "shining the light of
truth." As I said from the beginning, an addiction will thrive in
darkness, and the light is necessary if you're going to fight it.

Priests

Your regular confessor, who might also agree to be your
spiritual guide, can make a great accountability partner. You
could even kill two birds with one stone, if you met with him
personally (as opposed to over the phone). You could get your
confession in while giving your accountability report.

As mentioned earlier, priests have an awful lot of insight
when it comes to sin. And as an added bonus, they're guided by
the Holy Spirit in a way that other men aren't.

But I wouldn't recommend this route for several reasons:

1. You're not likely to find a priest who will agree to it.
    Priests are spread pretty thin right now. Their burdens are
    heavy, and they just don't have a lot of time on their
    hands. So don't be too disappointed if you ask one and he
    says no. In fact, many people have a hard time just finding
    one to serve as a spiritual director. A priest knows how
    limited his time is and would probably feel it's unfair to
    commit to something he couldn't do.

2. If you were lucky enough to find a priest who agreed to be an accountability partner, he probably still couldn't give you the time that an accountability partner needs to give. Unless he has a special gift like Padre Pio, and he can be in two places at once, he's probably spread pretty thin as it is.

3. It's usually better if an accountability partner is closer to your own realm—someone who is in the thick of family life, work routine, and who won't make you feel as though you're talking to someone 'above' you.

If you do use a priest as an accountability partner, I would suggest finding another one who isn't a priest and use them both.

Other Men

Generally, you find that other men, with lifestyles similar to yours, and who have a certain zeal for helping someone through addiction, serve as the best accountability partners. You might not be able to find such a person in the normal group of men you associate with. In fact, you might have a hard time finding someone who even understands how much pornography has ruined in your life. Most of your friends might think it's 'no big deal'. Even if they understood how destructive it is, they might not understand how much you've become dependent on it... how drawn you are to it even though you want to quit.

If you have a recovering alcoholic or drug addict in your circle of friends, this might make an ideal partner. Then you can be accountable to him and he can be accountable to you. Even though you don't suffer from the same addictions, you both understand trigger and temptation. You both understand the destructive powers that you're trying to escape.

But ultimately, another sex addict is probably your best bet. And the best place to meet one would be at a 12-step program like Celebrate Recovery or Sexaholics Anonymous. If your Catholic parish has something available, all the better.

Online

You can also turn online. There are quite a few forums available for pornography addicts. But at the same time, this poses two different problems.

First of all, the people you meet lack the face-to-face encounter you'd experience from a friend or 12-step partner. I can't stress the importance of this relationship enough. Online encounters and friendships have been growing vastly in the past ten years. But online friends, like pen pals, aren't the same as the people you meet regularly in person. There's a certain intimacy that's lacking. You might argue that even a husband and wife could meet through the internet. I would argue that they couldn't sustain a marriage through the internet.

Second of all, it means you'd be spending more time on the computer... which is one of the things that have drawn most pornography addicts into their imprisonment. Most of us use computers in our daily lives, especially at work. As you'll see in Chapter 7, it's time to eliminate as many temptations in your life as possible, and adding computer time to your schedule means adding temptation—not eliminating it.

One more quick note about online activity. I've joined a number of online communities and programs for sex addicts. Most of the people there (especially those who are advanced in their recoveries) agree on one thing: the online communities are not enough. You need something more—something personable.

Who Else To Tell

As mentioned earlier, you don't want to get caught up in exposing your problem to anyone and everyone. Mentioning it, even if it's part of your past and you've overcome it, should still give you a sense of shame. Both St. Augustine and St. Thomas Aquinas call lust the most shameful of all vices:

*"Now men are most ashamed of venereal acts, as
Augustine remarks (De Civitate Dei ("The City of God") xiv,*
74

18), so much so that even the conjugal act, which is adorned by the honesty [Cf. Q[145]] of marriage, is not devoid of shame: and this because the movement of the organs of generation is not subject to the command of reason, as are the movements of the other external members."[18]

This is a healthy attitude towards sex. We don't discuss it in front of just anyone. We have to develop, if we haven't already, a sense of social and spiritual privacy on the matter. But at the same time, because this vice has become such a monster in your life, it cannot remain completely secret. Now it's time to discuss who to tell and who not to tell about your problem. And the first one we'll talk about is the one whom many men fear telling most: their spouse.

Your Spouse

Perhaps your spouse already knows, and this is the easy part of this book. But most men have endured this addiction in total secrecy, and not even their wives have any clue about it. To them, the very worst thing in all the world is that their wives find out what they've become. At the same time, they almost pray that their wives somehow find out, because they know they can't quit until that happens. They fight with the idea almost as much as they fight with the pornography itself.

First of all, I won't say that you absolutely have to go tell your wife right now. Actually, it's not always advisable. You don't know how she will react. You don't know if, mentally, she can even handle it. But before we get into that, you should know one thing: I don't know of anyone with a long-time recovery record who *hasn't* told his wife.

---

[18] Summa Theologica Q146 A4 – Of Chastity

Jesus said that when you look at another woman with lust, you have already committed adultery with her in your heart. This addresses the *sin* of lust, and how it affects the soul. Now I'm going to take it one step further. When you look at another woman with lust, you've already committed adultery with her *in your wife's mind*. That's how many women take it, anyway. Not all of them do, and not all of them say so. But when you tell your wife what's been hidden from her for so long, she will very literally feel as though you've been having one affair after another. If you want to know what her reaction will be, consider what it would be if you told her you'd been sleeping around.

Of course, many of the men reading this might have already escalated to the point of cybersex or even to actually having affairs. We'll address that in a minute. First, we need to consider what the possible ramifications are for coming clean.

What we'd like to hear is, "Oh honey, I didn't know you were struggling with this so much alone. Let me help you in this battle."

What we're afraid of hearing is, "Get out of my house you nasty pervert, and never come back. Don't even think about ever touching one of my children again." As well as a public announcement of your problem and the humiliating experience as you come face to face with all the people she told.

What you're likely to get is somewhere in between, but it will lean more toward what you're afraid of than what you want to hear. Either way, you might want to plan on having a place to live, because many men are banned from their homes for a least a short time. Not all of them, but many of them. And if she does want to kick you out, refusing to leave is *not* a very apologetic approach. She will need time to process everything you tell her, and there's nothing wrong with giving her that time. Remember, you sinned against her—not the other way around.

Now as for what to say to her, how to say it, and when to do it, that's something you'll have to decide for yourself. But here are a few general rules that will help you in your approach:

- Do it privately. Whether you do it in a letter or sit down and talk to her, make sure she's going to be able to have 'alone time' if she wants it. Don't do it in public. Don't do it when you know the kids will be around within the next few hours.

- Be apologetic. Chances are, because of your addiction, you've already become very distant from your wife. This is one of those times where it helps to show you're still human—still capable of feeling. And sorrow is what you should be feeling. It doesn't hurt to show it.

- Don't fight her initial reaction. She might call you every name in the book. She might accuse you of things you *never* even thought of doing. It might be better, at this point, just to let her take out her anger on you and not fight back.

- Come TOTALLY clean. You've spent a number of years lying to her. If you hold back anything, you will just have to go through all of this again. And your chances of keeping your marriage together will be even smaller. If you've had affairs, tell her. If you've been frequenting strip clubs (or even hired prostitutes), tell her. If the pornography you've been looking at has escalated to something bizarre (or illegal), you'll have to tell her about that too. You don't want to go into specifics, like 'I masturbated to such and such picture', but she should have a very clear understanding of *what* she's dealing with and the problems she is now facing. Sometimes a complete list like this is better for a later conversation, like when she's decided to hear it. But don't put it off indefinitely. If you just tell her you're addicted to pornography, then tell her that when she's ready to talk (as in, 'when you feel like you want to hear it all'—leave it up to her) you can give her a more complete list of sins you've committed against her.

- Go to confession just before talking to her... and ask the priest for a blessing or prayer.
- **PRAY, PRAY, PRAY for guidance from the Holy Spirit.**

I can't stress this last one enough. If anyone can fix the situation, it's God. Don't rely on any of your own strengths or even your wife's mercy. Rely on God, and trust that He will bring good out of whatever happens. Pray for the right time. Pray for guidance in your approach to her. Pray for her. Pray for your children. Pray for everyone involved.

You might decide that, right now, your wife just couldn't handle it. Again, you know the situation better than anyone. So instead of telling your wife, you need to start praying about finding a right time. I don't mean say a quick prayer and then move on. I mean that it should be part of your daily prayers, one set aside from the others. You might be saying this prayer for a few weeks or for many years. But if you keep praying, God will eventually give you a way to tell her... and He will let you know when it's time.

Trust in God is a big factor in all of this. You've already learned that you can't trust yourself. And because of the nature of sexual addiction, you've probably conditioned yourself not to trust in others. The last one, the one you can never lose faith in, is God. If you don't feel like you trust God yet, then pray that you *learn* to trust Him. God is all knowing, all loving, and all good. You *must* find a way to reconcile with God before you can reconcile with anyone else.

Your Friends

Your normal group of friends (the male friends anyway) will probably have a mixed reaction if you tell them. Some might scoff, saying something like, "Whatever—we all look at porn. It's no big deal, man." Others might have been struggling with the same thing themselves. In fact, you might get more confessions from friends than you had planned. You might even find a friend willing to be an accountability partner.

Which friends you tell and which ones you don't tell is up to you... but it's probably better to at least tell the ones you spend the most time with, if you trust them to not announce it to the world.

The reason: because the men you spend the most time with (the ones who invite you over for movies or recommend certain media) can help you in your recovery if they know not to point you in the wrong direction. A good friend would not recommend a movie with nudity in it if he knows it would lead you into temptation. Nor would he invite you to page through his copy of Playboy if he knows you've decided to stand against that sort of thing. Nor will he be disappointed if you're watching a football game and you skip away from the commercials showing sexy women.

As mentioned earlier, you don't want to become too free with the public confessions. Not necessarily *all* of your friends need to know. And as a general rule, you should limit your confession to other men.

Other Women

Your wife is in a unique position. You are committed to her, not just physically and sexually, but emotionally as well. There are plenty of behaviors that are appropriate with your wife but aren't appropriate with other women. For example, crying on a woman's shoulder—this is something many would call an 'emotional affair.' A form of infidelity without physically cheating. Furthermore, sharing certain details (in fact, just about any detail) of your sex life with another woman would be equally inappropriate.

For this reason, you should limit yourself to men and your wife when sharing the details of your addiction. Discussion of sex with another woman is an openness God never intended.

But aside from being morally inappropriate, it's also a social mistake. Women will be creeped out by a man telling her he is a porn addict. She will be even more repulsed by any other details, such as masturbation. And rightly so. That is the socially acceptable response.

The very first thing Adam and Eve did after eating the forbidden fruit was to cover up their nakedness. They did this because sin causes a shame of sexuality. It's not like we can (or should try to) develop our natures to grow numb to this shame. A better understanding of sexuality doesn't change the nature of sexuality. It is something we should always guard, hide, and keep private. Especially with members of the opposite sex.

12 Step Programs

After prayer and the sacraments, joining a 12 Step program is probably going to be the next biggest aid in fighting your pornography addiction. Aside from the fact that they are specifically designed to combat the addict's lifestyle, they will help you network with other men. Men who understand what you're going through, who will help you through it, and who will ask for help in return.

G. K. Cesterton, in his book Man Alive, describes two types of men. One type surrounds himself with other men who are intellectually inferior. He draws satisfaction from being the on top. He is, in a sense, the big fish in a small pond. The other type surrounds himself with those he feels are superior. He gets satisfaction from their acceptance and from the challenge he faces while trying to 'impress' them.

Most of us do a combination of the two. We have men we look up to, and we look for their approval. We have other men we feel 'above' and we try to help them when we can. And, of course, we have a group of men we associate with that we feel equal to... usually one of them is our 'best friend.' This hierarchy is one created in our own minds, but it is real, all the same. It's just a fact of life.

In a 12 Step program, this hierarchy is eliminated. We are suddenly on a level playing field with men of all walks of life. This is probably one of the biggest reasons such programs work for men.

As you battle your addiction, you need two things: you need encouragement, and you need a sense of accomplishment in your victories. Women, for example, your wife, can offer this to a degree. But it will be far more effective if it comes from other men.

The men in your group are there because they have failed. They have been beaten by a behavior. They are there to battle themselves, and to beat the forces of a particular sin. In this kind of battle, the weak and lame can tower over the strong and vibrant. The intellectual peewee can outdo the intellectual giant. This is a battle of will and virtue. The same battle talked about throughout the Bible. There are no 'sure victories,' yet any one of us can take part in crushing the head of Satan. And we all cheer with enthusiasm for each other. We all help support our fallen soldiers. We all bring each other to Christ. Regardless of mental ability, physical stamina, financial position, or social stature. We all bring something to the table, we all receive something from the table.

Aside from this, a 12 Step program is the best place to find accountability partners. As you'll see in the later chapters, you'll need someone you can call on. Someone who will encourage you as you face temptation. You will absolutely need such a person as you try to piece back your life together. At first, you might feel overjoyed at being free from the sin. But eventually, that feeling of freedom will disappear, and you'll have to get back into the mundane routine of life. The temptation to sink back into the routine of sin will reappear, and might even be stronger than ever. Those are the times you'll need to pick up the phone and call a friend.

During the first few months of your recovery, you might even feel as though you don't need anything more. As though you've 'got the problem licked.' That is the time you should be looking for your trusted allies. Because the bigger storm is coming, and you want to be ready when the sky starts pouring and the thunder starts to roll.

Now let's go over our list:

1. You are recognizing and admitting to the wrongs you commit... as soon as you realize it.
2. You are praying every day.
3. You are confessing your sins to a priest in a reasonable amount of time.
4. You are giving an accountability partner scheduled updates.
5. You are being honest and apologetic with your spouse, without burdening her with details.

Chapter 7 – Change The Habit

A Christian man (we'll call him Joe) is invited to a party one night. He isn't happy at home, because of mounting bills or a dirty house or a hundred other reasons. He goes to the party, socializes a little, and has a few drinks. On that particular night, the beer has a very soothing effect. He feels comfortable—even lively. He feels, for the remainder of the party, as though everything is okay. Everything is manageable. The next night, his problems (the ones he felt so far away from) are still at his feet. He finds another party to go to—or even finds a bar where the same people frequent, if only to recapture that feeling of tranquility. Three months later, he's developed a habit—either go to the bar or bring home a six pack and drink it. He tells himself it's just a phase. Three years later, the habit is solidified. He gets grumpy and irritable if he doesn't go through the ritual each night. He's usually grumpy and irritable anyway. Three years after that, he finds he can hardly function without the ritual. Three years after that, the ritual has begun earlier and earlier each day—he now starts the process *while* he's at work. Three years after that, he cannot get through the morning without a drink.

Where did it start? It started with the first party. And yet, it would be incorrect to say that he never should have attended that party. It might even be incorrect to say that he shouldn't have gone to the bars. But on this we can all agree—if Joe wants to quit drinking, the people and circumstances surrounding his first drink need to be avoided at all costs.

I don't know what the circumstances are surrounding your first peek at the female body. It might have been a magazine. It might have been a catalog. It might have been the lady next door who jogs every morning wearing tight shorts and a half-top. But whatever it was, it slowly developed into a habit, and then to a mental and emotional dependency. In order to change that, you have to go back at the roots of your addiction, and avoid them at all costs. If you've failed to quit looking at pornography, it's probably because you failed to avoid the roots.

Killing The Roots Of Pornography Addiction

Pornography addiction, no matter what it's become to you, started with lust. It started with you looking at something you shouldn't look at. Jesus is very clear on this—if you lust after a woman, you are committing adultery with her in your heart. The way to break the addiction, among other things, is to stop looking at *all* women. The sexy joggers. The models in advertisements. The woman next door or at the office. The women in your favorite sitcom. The women in the chic-flicks your wife forces you to watch. All of them are off limits. Forbidden fruit. And remember, you don't take a bite of this kind of fruit by actually reaching out and taking it—you take a bite simply by looking at it.

The old adage "you can look, you just can't touch" is a LIE! Looking *is* touching.

I said from the beginning that this would be difficult. Despite the simplicity of the solution, I don't deny that it might be the most difficult thing you will ever do in your life. But it really is the answer. Yes, there are other things you'll have to do, but this will (after praying and asking for God's help) will be the determining factor. If you don't turn from *all* temptation, you will, sooner or later, find yourself on the computer again, pouring over thousands of pictures and videos.

There might have been a time when a man could sit and 'girl watch' in the park, and it never go any further than that, whether he's single or married. I won't argue about that, because it's a moot point for me and you. Right now, pornography is too easy to access—secretly, in the comfort of your own home or office.

But I would like to point out that the problem (girl watching developing into serious sins of lust) has been around for ages. Even before the time of Jesus. When Jesus spoke of 'looking at a woman with lust,' He wasn't coming up with a new notion.

Remember King David? Where did his big sin start? He was watching a woman take a bath. He was looking at forbidden fruit—something he had no right to do.

Controlling Your Eyes

When you look at a woman, any woman other than your wife, you must remember—you have no right to her. She is forbidden. When allowing your eyes to dance with her, you are violating her. Whether she wants you to or not (yes, I know—many women very deliberately dress so they attract our eyes), you still have no right to do it. When you do, you harm her, yourself, and your spouse. And mostly, you offend God.

From this day forth, every time you see the body of a women (except for your wife), you will shift your eyes away from her, saying to yourself, "She is forbidden."

We'll get into how to go about changing your habit of looking at women in the next section. For now, you at least have to commit. You have to promise God and yourself that this is your new goal—to completely stop looking at the bodies of other women.

You won't allow yourself to think about it or reason with yourself. There's nothing to say. There's no argument to have in your mind. She's forbidden—that's it. You don't need to see if she's wearing a specific kind of pants. You don't need to see if she's that one girl whom you met at a party. You don't need to see if she has a big butt or a small one. You don't need to see if she's a butter face. If you find yourself thinking about it— wondering if you should chance a second glance—then put a stop to such thoughts and repeat, "She is forbidden." Look away, stay away.

The first week you try this, you will be almost overcome by the amount of temptations you face each day. You will start to realize how much of your time you had once spent watching women. At times, you'll find yourself in a position where you have absolutely *nowhere* to rest your eyes. You look left, right, up, and down—everywhere there are women. Breasts, butts, faces, legs... they're everywhere.

Hang tight and remember—they are *all* forbidden fruit. Sometimes, it might even to be necessary to close your eyes for a time. A quick prayer can also help you get a handle on things.

As you practice this more, several other things will happen. Within a few months, it will become habit. As the Catechism tells us, this type of habit is a 'virtue':

> *A virtue is an habitual and firm disposition to do the good.*
> *It allows the person not only to perform good acts, but to*
> *give the best of himself. The virtuous person tends toward*
> *the good with all his sensory and spiritual powers; he*
> *pursues the good and chooses it in concrete actions.*[19]

Right now, you must force yourself to turn away from the female body —as in, you must have an actual thought process that leads you to do it. But within a short time (it usually only takes a few months) you will do it automatically... and you'll actually have to *force* yourself to take that second look.

Many men don't even believe this is possible. But not only is it possible, thousands of men have done it. Many men who have acquired the virtue of chastity simply allow their bodies to react, instead of having to rely on a decision each and every time they encounter temptation.

The secret to this is creating an actual, physical reaction to seeing a beautiful body.

Changing Routines and Patterns

We create routines and patterns in our lives all the time. For example, many of us get up in the morning, take a shower, and dress ourselves purely as a routine. We don't think about it.

---

[19] Catechism Of The Catholic Church, Article 1803

As we finish tying one shoe, we don't have to tell our bodies how to tie the next one. Our body does it on its own.

In the same way, we habitually look the female body up and down, drinking in her figure and beauty, and often storing it away for further meditation. By now, you've allowed it to become so much of a habit that you don't even realize you're doing it. It is a pattern, and it will take some time to break.

But it is important that we *do* break it, because our eyes open the doorway for lust. Lust cannot get a foothold without our sight. Every woman we see, no matter how modestly dressed she is, is an invitation to lust. We must break the pattern that our body uses to fill our heads with women to lust after.

Women

The key to breaking a pattern is replacing one action with another. You see a beautiful woman and instead of 'scanning' her for storage in your mind, you turn your head—180 degrees if you can, but at least make sure your neck muscles actually do some kind of work. That's not to say you have to keep your head turned. You can take one or two seconds, collect yourself, and then (if you *must* look at her at all) look into her eyes instead of down her shirt. Or simply point your line of sight somewhere else, and only allow her in your peripheral vision.

At first, this will seem awkward. You might even worry that it will draw attention. Ladies (whether at work or in the grocery store) might think you're personally trying to avoid them. Of course, you *are* trying to avoid them, but they don't have to know. Here are a few tricks to help make your pattern breaking skills look more inconspicuous:

- Suddenly stop and pat your pockets down, as if you think you might have forgotten something. Then look satisfied (after you've gotten your brain under control) and move forward again.

- Pull your phone out and look at it, as if you just got a text message... or wanted to read one you had gotten earlier.
- Look at your watch.
- Act as though something caught your eye—an airplane, a passing car, a weed in the grass... whatever.
- Carry a piece of paper with you (perhaps folded in your pocket) and pull it out, pretending to read a checklist.

This is the very first pattern you'll work to break. It is the key pattern, because all of the other lustful patterns stem from this one. The next pattern you'll work on is almost the same thing—except it concerns the media instead of actual women.

Television

We don't have control over what they broadcast on television. But we have control over what we watch. So the next time a beautiful body appears on your screen, you're going to turn it off, turn the channel, or fast forward it. And if you absolutely can't do any of these (for example, when you're at someone else's house) you're going to turn your head away—the same as if the girl is standing right in front of you.

In order to do this, you are always (I repeat—ALWAYS) going to have an alternative object to look at when you sit down to watch television. Here is a list of things you might try:

- **A Book** – Keep it out and open so that you can start reading it at any given time.
- **A Pen and Piece of Paper** – Maybe making a list or a note. You might just act like you enjoy doodling. I personally enjoy making mazes, since I'm not very artistic.
- **A Rubik's Cube** – These are especially good if you can find a pocket sized one, but any kind of 'pocket puzzle' will do.

- **Homework or Paperwork** – Of course, this would only work at home.
- **A Hobby** – There are a thousand hobbies you could pick up that you could do in front of the television. I used to make rosaries while watching TV.
- **Origami** – In the movie "Blade Runner", one of the cops would always take tissues, gum wrappers, or any piece of paper and twist them into different shapes. Something like this could be used anywhere at any time. All you need is a tiny piece of paper and some imagination.
- **Magnets** – I don't know why, but two magnets can hold a person's attention for an awful long time—and all you need to do is stay distracted until the scene change. Keeping a set in your pocket might draw a few questions, but it's certainly not going to blow your cover.

I'm sure you can think of a few more things. I know that at home, I always fold clothes while watching TV. It helps my wife and it offers a distraction whenever I need it. Do whatever you have to do, but make sure you never sit down to watch TV unless you have already arranged for a distraction. You should know what and where the distraction is before you start. It is an agreement with yourself.

As with the pattern of staring at women, your mind will try to reason itself into taking that second glance. Some might even say the devil will be tempting you directly with seductive arguments. *Was that such and such actress? Was she really that badly dressed—take a second look and see. Is the scene over yet—they probably aren't showing her from the same camera point now.*

Don't give such notions an audience. There's no reason to look. She's forbidden. Period. Tell yourself that and then think about something else. If you keep the conversation going, you'll lose. Don't try to do direct battle with the devil. Let St. Michael the Arch Angel do that. *You* run. Flee evil. That is your strategy, and it will never change.

Magazines

The first question I would ask is this: do you *really* need to read a magazine—any magazine—that has pictures of sexy women in it? Probably not. Not ones that make a definite point of having scantily clad women in them anyway. A lot of car and truck magazines just don't need your attention. So if you can, cancel your subscriptions to them and don't think about them again.

But let's face it, you can't very well help it if someone places a sexy ad in your favorite astrology magazine—or a gardening magazine or computer gadgets catalog or whatever. In cases like that, you can often get caught completely off-guard.

Here's what you do. When you first get the magazine, you flip through it while someone is in the room with you. Even if it's one of your kids or a coworker—they can be entirely unaware of what you're doing. Go through it page by page, but very quickly.

You remember how it was to go through a magazine, looking for sexy women. No matter how fast you were turning the pages, the flash of skin you saw alerted you, telling you to stop and look. Now it's going to help you locate the page, trying not to look directly at the image, and rip it out... crumbling it as you do, so that you can't quite see the page once it's in your hand. Then throw it away.

If someone asks you why you're doing that, simply tell them that you get tired of the publisher cluttering the articles with non-stop ads.

But what about all those magazines your wife (or daughter or mom) gets? The magazine covers themselves are a source of temptation. The ads and articles in them are downright sinful... for you anyway. How do you avoid that?

This is where it *really* helps if your wife is aware of your problem. Then you can make an agreement with her that if the front cover has a seductive image, she tears it off and tosses it.

That way, it won't constantly draw your attention. If your wife doesn't know, then always make it a point to have another book or magazine close to where she keeps hers. Every time you pass it, put your magazine over top of hers, so that the image isn't so inviting.

It would be even more helpful if all of the women's magazine and catalogs were in a specific area—one you won't ever visit. Your wife's underwear drawer would be a good spot.

Now as for those other catalogs and ads, the ones that are in the Sunday paper each week, you might ask your wife to tear out the lingerie section if you really feel you must look through them. But honestly, does the Sears catalog outdo the Home Depot, Best Buy, or even the HH Greg catalog? Couldn't you stand to just not look at the catalogs that include a lingerie section?

Enough said.

Let's get into the most difficult one of all.

The Internet

This is what trapped most men to begin with. Unfortunately, it's become such a huge part of our world, that most of us simply can't cancel our service and do without it entirely. It's become part of school, work, and even the bill payment process. It's here for good, and we need to learn how to deal with it.

Before we go into the patterns and routines, let's start with the fact that most of us spend *much* more time online than we have to. So we need to change the way we think about the computer. If you really want this to work, then you need to set some ground rules for yourself:

1. The computer is a tool. You work on it, you keep track of finances, you write, you design video games, you do business. Whatever it is you *need* the computer for, you

must always think of it as a tool to accomplish that—especially when you are alone.

2. The computer (while you are alone) is *not* a source of entertainment. You don't need to see the latest YouTube video. You don't need to read the latest email forward. These are the things that make you think of the computer as a source of entertainment. And when the latest YouTube video is no longer funny, your mind will want to find something equally amusing. It will want porn.

3. If possible, you will *not* be online while alone.

4. If possible, you will have every computer with internet access filtered (we'll talk about this more in the chapter on purifying your home).

5. Your computer will be stationed in an area where lots of cross-traffic happens... and EVERYONE can see the computer screen.

I understand that you can't make *all* of these changes. There are some people whose entire living depends on being online, in a private office, on a computer that is completely unfiltered. If this is you, changing your approach to the online world is going to be very difficult. When your work is physical labor, you need breaks. You need breaks from mental labor also. And during those breaks, if you can't *leave* the computer, you will be drawn to the very thing you're trying to escape.

I would, however, submit this idea: is this a job you've trained for your whole life and are committed to, or would it be possible to make a career change? I'm not trying to push anyone, because I have no idea what your situation is. But eventually you might have to take a hard look at what's worth more to you—your career (if you can't make enough changes to break this addiction) or your soul.

After you've set as many ground rules for yourself as possible (the first two being the most important ones) it's time to work on the patterns themselves. And there are times that they are more than just patterns—some of them have become rituals.

Like with the other patterns we're working on, the first thing you'll need is a physical response to temptation. But we're not just going to look away when a sexy woman pops up on the screen. That wouldn't work very well, since the woman will still be there until you, the user, actually exit that screen out. And besides, the biggest temptation online isn't always an image. It's often a certain website (or number of them) that you frequent. Forums, YouTube, chat sites, stock image sites, Google image searches—they've all ensnared a great number of men.

The fact is, *you* know which sites draw you in the most. So I couldn't possibly make a list of the sites that you are no longer allowed to visit. But you should make such a list for yourself.

Watching online porn doesn't always have a direct route. You might visit a more family friendly site and then click through a series of links that eventually take you down the rabbit hole. But there is a point, isn't there, in which you know where you're headed—at least, you know where you'll *probably* end up.

It starts with one click or one search. You know where it's going and your body begins to prepare for it. Increased heart rate and breathing. Tingling in your belly or extremities. Your head swimming. You know you've taken the first step and your body is already anticipating the final plunge. This is called pursuing. You're trying to find temptations. You're pursuing a sin.

If you haven't been able to clean up for more than a day, you might not experience this every time. Your body may, by now, be numb to the 'thrill.' But you still know when you've crossed the line. There is a border around that slippery slope, and we know immediately when we've decided to slip under the yellow warning tape.

THAT is where you're going to change the pattern. The very first click you make or search term you type. It's different for a lot of men. But you know where it is for you.

For example, let's say you normally start with YouTube, and then start clicking on the sexier videos, and then start actually searching for sexier videos, and then move on to a more explicit site. YouTube is the starting point. That's where you are NOT going to go. Not ever again.

You can start by erasing all the bookmarks and favorite links that you know lead you to those 'first step' sites. Get rid of all of them (including emails that friends sent you with links to them) and don't think about it again. You have to do most of this stuff without thinking or you'll argue you way into holding on to something that will make you fall.

From now on, as you start typing in "youtube.com" in the browser address bar, you're going to stop yourself, put your arms down, and scoot back from the computer... before you even finish typing the whole address.

For a while, it might even be good to turn completely around, and if you're able to, get up and walk away from the desk. This is your physical response to the first step of your ritual—to flee.

If you happen to already have a window open, or you're struggling with an ad and you want to click on it, you might have to exit the window, so that it's not staring at you when you return to the computer. But get away from it fast and give your mind time to recover. Go to a place where you can think straight. Maybe it's the water cooler. Maybe it's the cubicle next to you where you can chat with a coworker. Do whatever you have to, but get away from the temptation until you've collected your thoughts and are ready to use the computer as a tool again and not as a source of entertainment. If you were only on the computer for entertainment and don't actually need to do something, then don't go back to the computer at all. Hit the power button as you leave.

One last thing before we move on: sometimes we try to justify overuse of the internet by spending time on Christian based sites. I've done it. I know a lot of other guys who do it. You might spend fifteen minutes on a Catholic forum. Then you might go back and see if anyone replied to you. Then you might read a few Catholic blogs, commenting on each. Then you have to go check both to see if anyone responded to your responses. You might even get into a heavy discussion or debate, and think that your attention is needed for the salvation of someone's soul.

Don't let yourself fall for that. What you're really doing is training your mind to accept the internet as a place of interaction and entertainment (you wouldn't be doing it if it wasn't entertaining to you—even if you're arguing with someone about politics or religion). You can waste vast amounts of time while you do this. And eventually, when your mind gets bored with it, you will search for other ways to fill that time—usually it will lead you back to porn. That's just the way it happens, and there's nothing you can do about it. If you want to break the habit for good, you *must* stop using the computer to entertain yourself.

Mobile

A lot of people thought we had too much screen time when televisions became a household item. We all realize we get too much screen time now that computers are household items. But as laptops and smartphones gain popularity, it's almost scary the way people are becoming obsessed with electronic entertainment.

When I was younger, my friends and I made it a point to get together every two months for a friendly poker game. As our families and responsibilities grew, we had to cut down on poker nights. Finally, we stopped all together. Then, years later, we decided to get together one more time. There were five guys. Three of them stopped more than once to read emails on their phones. Not one of them were 'on call' or waiting for some kind of important news. They were simply acting out of habit.

You see what happened? We're all there to play poker and BS together. That, in itself, is a source of entertainment. One we all enjoyed. There was absolutely no need for other entertainment. Not only did the phones encroach on the evening, it also pulled the men out of their social circle, isolating them.

This kind of isolation is causing more and more men to dive into pornography. And they're doing it in open areas, surrounded by people, isolating themselves even when they aren't alone. This makes mobile phones (the ones that can receive and send messages) a dangerous component in pornography addiction. The fact that a man can isolate himself so much, and feed that isolation so easily, is troubling.

The first thing I'll say is this: regular cell phones (the kind that simply make phone calls) are still available... along with plans that do not include data transfer (texts and images). If your job does not absolutely require you to have a smartphone, then you should switch to a simple cell phone and get rid of the extra garbage that's keeping you bound to a life of sin.

This might be hard for you to accept—especially if you've allowed it to become a big part of your life. But it's something you *must* accept. If you keep the data transfer, it will probably bring you down. I've talked to so many men out there, who were clean for long lengths of time, and then who slowly slipped into the darkness again because of smartphones.

But some men can't do this. If your company requires you to have a phone with unlimited (and unfiltered) online access, then you're going to have to work very hard to change the way you use it. You'll use basically the same approach we went over for the computer.

The phone is a tool—nothing more. You must disassociate phone usage with entertainment. Every time you use the phone, you must have a very specific plan for what you're doing. No more browsing or searching or surfing. You use it to communicate with someone specific, to make notes or entries in a specific app, or you don't use it at all... you don't even take it out to look at it. Period.

Many men find that their communications are specifically what draws them into the pornography. Notices from joke sites, email forwards from friends, spam, etc.,.

You're going to have to go through each of these and cleanse them. In fact, if you can change your email address or phone number, then that might be the best first step you can take. But it would only be your *first* step.

Read through Chapter 8 on changing your life for more specifics on how to deal with incoming temptations from friends on your phone.

As with computers, there is a line you cross when you are diving into your pornography ritual. It could be a site, an email from a specific person, a bookmark, or a set of links that lead you deeper into the rabbit hole. But you know as you look at it what's happening, and you know that eventually, it will lead to you watching porn and masturbating.

You must stop at the very first step. That first email, image search, or website. As you approach the line, you have to keep yourself from crossing it.

Turn the phone off, and put it in your pocket.

That is your new routine. Every time you see or sense temptation, that will be your reaction. You can get it back out again after you've collected yourself. It might be immediately, it might be a half hour. But you must power that phone down. You must give yourself those few moments that it would take for the phone to reboot. You're not going to miss anything major during that time. If your boss complains about something, you can make plenty of excuses. It's my understanding that those phones get stuck on stupid sometimes anyway and must be rebooted. So just do it and deal with the consequences.

As with all the other pattern changes, you cannot give yourself time to think. You cannot give audience to Satan. You cannot make excuses for yourself. Just do it, without thought. You're working on a habit now, and habits (by definition) do not require thought.

If you can set your mobile browser to go back to a home page when you first turn it on, great. Some will automatically go back to the last page you looked at, which means the temptation will be there again just as soon as you reboot the phone. That's why you have to take those few minutes and actually power down—because it will give you enough time to build the strength you need to exit the browser or delete the email without looking at it further.

Baths and Showers

For just a second, we're going to switch focus. As I had said earlier, the temptations enter into us through our eyes. But even if we starve our eyes, the temptation to masturbate (with or without pictures) can sometimes be very strong—especially in the bathtub. As you do with the temptation to stare, you're going to develop a new reaction to the temptation to masturbate in the bath.

First, you're going to make some rules for yourself. If you have a problem in the bathroom, then you need a time limit. It shouldn't take you any longer than five minutes to shower, dry, and (at least partially) dress. So that's all you're going to give yourself. In fact, if you can, you're going to put a timer in the bathroom. As soon as you are finished adjusting the water, before you even take the towel off, you're going to set the timer for five minutes.

Then get in.

You're also going to change the soap you use. I realize not every man can do this, as some have reactions to harsh soaps, but the majority of you can. You're going to stop using soaps that smell feminine. Use something that won't make you think of a woman—something that smells masculine.

If your skin can tolerate it, you're also going to switch to a gritty soap—something with pumice in it that feels harsh and scratchy. Something made to cut grease when you work on cars. Lava hand soap is good. There are also gritty body washes that can work well. You might have to do a little shopping.

If you feel yourself being tempted, you're going to turn the water off. Even if you're right in the middle of rinsing shampoo out of your eyes. Turn it completely off and count to ten. Then turn it back on and start over. If you start the shower again with cold water, and give your body that 'cold shock', it might help you even more.

Continue with your shower and finish before the timer goes off.

Hotels

This is a biggie for many men—those who travel a lot anyway. At one time, it was just the loneliness that got to men. But then they started serving men cable TV (whether they asked for it or not). Then came the movies on demand, where you can watch XXX rated movies without anyone even knowing (it comes up as a simple 'entertainment fee' or something on the bill). The final blow was when internet connection to each room became a standard. Now, it's impossible for a man *not* to be tempted when he's traveling alone.

Let's start with the television. When you first get to your room, before you hang up a single article of clothing, reach behind the TV and unplug it. Don't argue yourself into turning it on at all—not to watch the news or your favorite sitcom or anything else. Just leave it unplugged and it won't be a problem. When you're watching TV, it's way too easy to happen to flip by the movie channels and 'see what's playing'. It's a little harder to get out of bed and reach around the TV so you can plug it in. That will give you time to think about what you're doing and squash the temptation.

If you have a laptop, then leave it in the car.

You have some work you need to complete on the laptop. Here's how you handle that. First of all, you designate the time you're going to work. Make that time as early as you possibly can. You want to get the work done before you start to feel 'finished' for the day. As soon as you're done, lock the computer back in your car.

If you can do your work in the lobby or at a restaurant, then you'll alleviate a huge part of the temptation. That way you won't even have to bring the laptop into your hotel room. But if that isn't an option, you might try setting the computer up with your back to the door... so that if someone opened the door they could see the computer screen as plain as day. Then (yes, this is might seem a little overboard, but it does actually work) prop the door open. Anyone passing an open door in a hotel room will naturally look inside. You'll keep that in mind as you work and won't be nearly as tempted to look at anything inappropriate.

And then, once you've finished your work, wrap up the computer and lock it away in your car. Once you've finished your work, there's no reason to have it with you. Not alone in a hotel room anyway.

Again, you'll want to argue yourself out of these things. Don't give audience to the voice of Satan. There's nothing to talk about. There's nothing to reason against. You must tell yourself, "I'm going to do it this way and that's that."

Avoiding Temptations

Now that we've spelled out the ways you'll deal with temptations, let's discuss some of the ways to avoid those temptations all together. This will be especially important during the first few months of your recovery. In fact, you'll *have* to be much more strict at first. You might be able to relax some of the rules later; but even then, you don't want to fall into complacency.

*Read more about complacency in Chapter 11 on avoiding traps.

We had mentioned earlier that pornography is a unique problem in that the temptation is literally *everywhere*. A drunk can avoid bars. A gambler can avoid casinos. But you cannot avoid women—not completely anyway. And every woman you look at can be a source of temptation.

However, there are plenty of places that put you in a special state of excitement. Places that, for instance, have many women—women who are dressed appropriately but provocatively. For example, the gym. The women there aren't necessarily showing too much body as they exercise in their leotards. It isn't their fault that you can't control your eyes.

Perhaps the world would be a better place if leotards didn't exist and all women wore ugly sweat suits to work out. But really—wouldn't that change the nature of women? We love women because they are beautiful. They enjoy being beautiful. They do what they can to make themselves beautiful, even when they are doing something that makes them sweaty and smelly. We have to accept that. Besides, even if it were wrong, there's nothing we can do about the way our culture is. Women dress sexy. If this is tempting to us (and I don't know many men who aren't tempted by it) then we must react appropriately and not try to shift the blame on them.

The answer—don't go to a gym where women work out.

For men who are really into physical fitness, I can already hear the arguments. I'm not going to waste time refuting them. You know that it's a temptation; you know you shouldn't be there. Switch gyms or stay at home to work out. You're no longer worshipping your old gods—whether it's sex or physical fitness. Your new God is the real one. Serve Him, and don't let anything get in the way.

Of course, gyms aren't the only places you should avoid. Public pools and beaches are also a problem spot for guys. And they're not as easy to avoid as gyms. Especially if you have a wife and kids who expect you to take them there.

If you can, you should find a way to send your kids to the beach without you. It might even be something you should discuss with your wife. "Honey, for now, all the bikinis are creating a problem. I will get to a point where I can deal with them, but I need a few months to create new habits—to change the way I react to them. Can you give me that time?"

Some men have a specific place that would ordinarily be completely innocent—but for them has become a feeding ground for their behavior. Especially men who have escalated to voyeurism.

For example, you might sit in the park for hours watching mothers care for their children. You don't follow them home or anything. You don't try to attack them. You don't take it any further than watching—except in your own mind.

If this is your problem spot, then this is the very place you need to avoid. Unless it's a place that you *must* go (because of a job requirement or because you're obligated to take your kids or wife there), then you need to stop going.

You might also have to drive to work and other places by a different route. Let's say, for example, you frequented a strip club on your way home from work—or even during your lunch break. You might be able to drive past it without being tempted to visit it. But doesn't seeing it (just seeing the blocked windows and big steel door) activate something in your mind? Doesn't your imagination take you places you shouldn't be? Aren't the images driving you to seek something more—either at home or some other private place? Change your route so you don't have to see it at all. Why put yourself through more temptation? Avoid your temptation spots, and make your recovery that much easier.

Billboards are also a big temptation for men. I've seen some billboards that are downright pornographic. It would be nice if our culture had developed a sense of decency and such advertisements didn't exist. But they are there, and the only reaction we can have is to avoid them. If a billboard is a heavy temptation to you, then try another route. If you can't, you might try taking a drink of your morning coffee (or whatever else you have) as you pass the danger zone.

In Chapter 8 on purifying your home, we'll discuss what to do with all the movies and shows with sensuality in them. For now though, while you're developing a physical reaction to tempting images, it's best that you watch very little television at all. In fact, if you can *not* watch any, you'd be doing yourself a big favor. Eventually, you'll have to grow into the right approach to television. But you must spend some time starving your eyes of sensuality before you can handle what has become routine lifestyle. So a few months of totally avoiding the TV would be best. Spend that time with a hobby, reading, or doing what you've been missing during your pornography obsession... spend it working on your relationships with your wife, kids, friends, and other family.

You might have to avoid specific women. Maybe one you've had a crush on and have spent time fantasizing about. Even if your fantasies aren't sexual.

102

This is especially important for married men. Again, the draw of pornography is the escapism from reality. Part of that reality is your commitment to your wife and children. If there is a high school crush that has come back into your life, if you received an email from an attractive woman, if you are frequenting a restaurant where the waitress seems receptive to your flirts—you *must* cease all contact with her. She is drawing you away from your commitment. She is keeping you from having a full relationship with your wife. No more visits. No more conversations. No more Facebook pokes. No more flirtatious emails. No more daydreams. Turn your body, mind, and attention to the one God gave you to cherish—your wife. Even when she's mad at you or you're mad at her.

Controlling Your Thoughts

As strange as it may seem, your body is easy to control—your mind is a little more difficult. Your body, after conditioning it, will immediately turn from temptation without having a thought process. Your mind won't respond quite so easily.

For example, when was the last time you've been able to say a rosary (or even an entire Hail Mary) without being distracted? For most men, that would be never. In fact, your thoughts change subjects so quickly that it's rarely possible for you to stay focused on one single thing for more than a few minutes. And even then, outside thoughts (ones stemming from unrelated subject matter) constantly bombard you, whether you give them audience or not.

However—there is one subject that we all seem to be able to focus on, without losing any train of thought, for a very long time. That subject is sex. Especially if we're feeding our attention with hundreds of pornographic pictures, whether from a computer screen or from memory.

The trick you'll have to learn is to distract your mind from sex the way it is distracted from everything else. Sometimes, you'll have to enter several levels of consciousness. Not to sound like a mystic but we all know that we can do one thing with our hands, do another thing with our imaginations, and still another with our conscious thoughts. For example, I might drive with my body (seeing and reacting to everything on the road), pray the rosary with my mind (trying my hardest to meditate on the mysteries), and still somehow manage to think about the girl I just passed (even if it's only for a few seconds).

Don't Think Pink

Once someone says, "Don't think pink," you have no choice but to think pink. The only way to stop thinking pink, is to think another color like blue or green. To escape impure thoughts, you have to change focus. You have to think another color.

Sometimes it's impossible to *not* think about sex. Especially when so much of our culture is screaming it at you. This very book could be an enormous amount of temptation. The only way you can effectively battle this temptation is by directly changing your focus onto something else. Something that will absorb your attention, on more than one level.

Prayer and meditation is a wonderful tool. And the rosary is one of the easiest to say. Even if you don't say a whole rosary, you can still say one decade—or even half a decade. You might also try the Chaplet of Divine Mercy, meditating on the sorrowful mysteries as you pray with your mouth.

It's also helpful to think about the general mysteries of our faith—with or without repeating memorized prayers. The great part about the mysteries is that you can think about them, discover them, and grow in your understanding of them without ever completely exhausting the discoveries they hold. It's like drawing from the everlasting well of God's divine light. You'll never stop learning about them. You'll never be left with old, sour thoughts that have lost their novelty...

But in the moments of temptation, you will have a hard time thinking of what to distract yourself with. And the mysteries you've spent so much time thinking about suddenly don't seem so mysterious anymore—as if they've lost their flavor and intrigue.

Having A List Of Distractions

For this reason, it's good to always carry a list of distractions. I've compiled a short list of religious mysteries, questions, and meditations for you to draw from, but the list is by no means exhaustive. There are many more, possibly ones that draw your interest better than these.

1. The story of the good thief, who hung on the cross next to Christ in Luke 23:39-43. What could his crime have possibly been? Why did he decide, in his last moments, to come to Jesus? Isn't it interesting that a criminal was the only one ever recorded to have received one of the greatest promises ever: to be with Christ, *that very day,* in paradise? Was it because he was the only one suffering with Christ as they hung on the cross?

2. What was Paul talking about when he said a thorn bothered him in 2 Corinthians 12:7-10? Was he talking about sins he had committed or a weakness he was prone to? Had he fallen to that weakness?

3. How can Jesus be God completely and entirely, if there are three persons in God?

4. What significance did the Samaritan woman have in John 4:3-42? Why did Christ choose to reveal so much of Himself to her?

5. Who was the paralytic who had been lowered through the roof and healed by Jesus in Mark 2:1-12? Did he have something specific he wanted to be forgiven for? Did he, as well as the townspeople, believe his physical problem was due solely to a sin? What does that mean for me? Do I believe all of my limitations and afflictions are due to past sins? If Jesus forgives me, will my problems disappear? If so, why didn't they disappear for the saints?

As I said, religious distractions don't always work. You're not working toward an end goal, and sometimes deep thought without an actual goal in mind or solution to be reached is tedious. And sometimes it will not distract you at all.

For this reason, it's also good to have (whether in your mind or on a piece of paper) a list of brain teasers and riddles that you haven't quite solved yet. They might be mathematical equations (if you're able to solve such things in your mind), word problems, or just mechanical theory questions. Perhaps it's something you already know the answer to, but want to behold the solution entirely in your mind... to understand all parts of it at once, even though there are several layers or steps to the solution.

For example, I once struggled with a series of gears in an envelope inserter machine. I could picture the schematic in my head. I could picture the actual machine in my head. I knew what had to be done if X gear was turning the wrong way or was not turning at all. But I couldn't all at once picture the movement of all parts, their relationship to each other, and how they eventually affected the non-rotating gear. And every time I found myself struggling with sexual thoughts, I jumped back on that problem again. It literally took all of my attention to resolve it. And this distracted my mind from temptation.

This was work related—something I was very close to. But it doesn't have to be. Here's a very short list of riddles you might try to work out. Don't think about them unless you're being tempted. Remember, the goal is not to find the answers (which are readily available on many websites) but to distract your mind. Once you realize your thoughts are a safe distance from temptation, stop thinking about them so that you'll still have fire power the next time temptation arises.

1. Your friend draws a straight line in the sand, and says, "Make the line shorter without erasing any part of it." How do you do it?

2. Make the number 17 out of an equation using the numbers 1, 2, 6, & 7. Only use each number once and you must use all of them. There are several answers. You can find more "number riddles" online.
3. A man stands in one spot. The only direction he can see is south, no matter which way he turns. A bear approaches him. What color is the bear?
4. A bus driver goes south on Main St. He goes through a stop sign without stopping. He goes the wrong way on a one way street. He went left at a 'no left turn' sign. But he didn't break a single law. Why not?
5. What in an engine serves no purpose but without it the engine doesn't work?

These are just a few, and there are a million more. You can find them online, but I would suggest getting a book of riddles. Look up the answers for the first few of them to see if the book is any good. Let's face it, some riddles are stupid. Either the answer is not obtainable from the information given, or the answer is too obvious. After you're sure it's a good book of riddles, buy it, tear out a page, and keep it in your pocket. When you've got all the answers on that page, compare them with the answers in the back of the book, and then move on to the next page.

Riddles aren't the only way to distract your mind. You might have a thousand ways to do it. The point is to have a distraction available at all times. Know what it is *before* you get hit with mental images, so that you always have something to fall back on.

Now let's go over our list:

1. You are recognizing and admitting to the wrongs you commit... as soon as you realize it.
2. You are praying every day.

3. You are confessing your sins to a priest in a reasonable amount of time.
4. You are giving an accountability partner scheduled updates.
5. You are being honest and apologetic with your spouse, without burdening her with details.
6. You have specific responses to specific temptations, you know what they are, and you practice them constantly.
7. You don't think about your response—you just do it.

Chapter 8 – Change Your Life

Even if you've followed all the directions in this book up till now, it's still not enough to keep you entirely away from pornography. Changing your habits, coming back into the Church, and sharing your struggles with someone isn't good enough. You have to change your lifestyle as well. That means changing the things in your home and office. It means changing the way you speak. It means changing the way you approach people. Sometimes, it can even mean saying goodbye to old friends... although usually it doesn't come to that.

Many of these changes will happen naturally, without specific effort on your part. But it's important to know that they're there, and to know that they coincide with purity. For example, you should notice a change in your conversation patterns. Since you've stopped staring at passing girls, you'll stop nudging your friends in the ribs and saying, "Look at that rack." And when they say it, it will throw you into a little bit of a loop. You shouldn't engage in such conversation. That's not to say you should insult or correct anyone. But the more you talk about it, the more you'll think about it, the more you'll want to look at it. Then your recovery falls apart. So don't give audience to the temptations to comment on women. Just let it go and change the conversation... without thinking about it.

This and many changes will happen. Allow the changes, and feed the new sense of purity. But aside from those that happen by themselves, you'll have to take some very definite steps to clean your lifestyle. And it all starts in the home.

Purifying Your Home

Purifying your home is one thing that will be a whole lot easier if your wife knows about your problem. In fact, she'll probably be all too willing to help you. Because purifying your home, to her, will be like giving the boot to 'the other woman' who was destroying her marriage.

But at the same time, it will probably cause some not-so-good reactions from her. Up until now, your wife might not have understood just how serious a pornography addiction is. If you tell her that the exercise videos she watches are a temptation for you (or even that the girl on the DVD cover is a temptation), her feelings may be crushed. She'll get the feeling that *every* woman is now competing with her. That you can't go through a day without being drawn sexually to another woman. There's no real answer for this, but you should at least be aware that she could feel this way.

In the event that you haven't been able to come clean with your spouse, you can still make some huge changes in your home. And those changes will probably make your spouse feel better about your relationship, even if she doesn't know why you're doing it.

Let's start with the media in your house. The electronic as well as printed stuff. Everything with nudity has to go. All of your R-rated (and even the PG-13) goes to the trash. Every magazine with scantily clad women, whether you enjoy the articles or not, goes. Don't leave anything behind.

Why throw it away? Why not just sell it on Ebay or give it to a friend?

Think about the Old Testament. God demanded that those faithful to Him offer Him sacrifices. Specific sacrifices. He didn't just make them up. He wasn't demanding certain animals because He fancied one more than another. God wanted certain animals sacrificed because He knew that many of His people had fallen into the evil practices of the Gentiles. His people were worshipping the images and statues of bulls, sheep, and birds. **So God demanded that they kill those very animals, burning them so that they were no longer useful to humans**. It was a statement from God. "Prove to me that you will always hold me higher than those false gods you worshipped—put me above them!"

That's what you're going to do. You're going to commit yourself to your new God—the real God. The false gods you've been worshipping for years are going to be burned and offered up in sacrifice. You need to do it this way. You have to plunge the dagger deep into the heart of your false god.

So throw it away. If your wife asks about it (and you haven't told her yet) then you can simply say that you have made a commitment to purity—and that these movies, magazines, books, etc., are against that oath. Probably, she'll be happy about it rather than upset.

As you do this, don't be surprised if you feel a certain sense of liberation—of freedom after a long, hard bondage. That's what it is—freedom. You're telling Satan that he no longer holds the leash. You're giving him what-for. Be proud as you do it, and let yourself soak in a little glory. It won't last long, but it's nice while it's there.

Now for your computer. If there's anything on there—if you had made it a habit to store images on your hard drive—then you need to format. Don't try to go through each folder and find all the garbage you've collected. Just start fresh. Only back-up the specific files that you need. Use the installation disk you were provided when you first bought the computer. If you don't know how, then plead and beg whichever friend you have that is the most computer-literate.

Next, install filters on your computer. You can find some pretty good filters online—both free and subscription software. I prefer K9 because it's free. This is especially helpful if your wife knows about your problem and might check up on you every once in a while without notice. If your wife doesn't know yet, you can use still use K9 because it also guards against fraudulent websites (phishing sites). If your wife doesn't check up on you, then make sure your accountability partner or sponsor can.

But beware—you *cannot* depend on computer filters to block out everything. A well filtered computer will still not keep you from looking at pornography. Some people install them (whether it's for their kids or for themselves) and think they can relax. Filtering a computer might give you a little time to think about what you're doing, but it definitely won't replace self-discipline. It's a tool, but don't make the mistake of relying on it.

As you eliminate more of the sexual clutter in your life and as you starve your eyes of sensuality, you're going to start digging in some of the most unlikely places for images. You might go through an entire day without looking at a single woman. But as you check your email in the evening, you'll look forward to 'accidentally' glancing at the pictures of women in all the various illicit ads (SPAM).

The easiest and safest way to avoid it is to just break away from your old electronic identity and enjoy a clean, new one.

Change your email address. I know, it's a pain to send out emails to all your friends and contacts... and even then, half of them will continue to use your old one. But if you're getting obscene spam, and it creates a problem for you, then it has to be done.

How do you know if it's necessary? Think back—have you ever sifted through your spam, looking for images? If so, then you have to do this.

If it's been a problem for you, you might also have to change your mobile number. If you're using a mobile from work, you could probably get away with telling your boss that your number somehow got on a text spam list and that you're having trouble sorting through all the messages.

Now for your home-based workshop. The garage, the basement, the 5-foot corner of one room—wherever it is. You have to clean that out as well. That means throwing away the bikini calendar and posters. It means getting rid of all the joke comics (the ones with sexual punch lines) hanging up. It means that if someone were to walk into your shop, they would understand that foul language would be out of place there. That doesn't mean you have to put up religious statues all over the place (although it wouldn't hurt you). It just means it should be considered a place where purity can flourish.

Purifying Your Workplace

A place of work *should* be easier to clean than the home. After all, your employer would want to maintain a comfortable

112

and professional setting, right? One that would be inviting for clients—even if they don't often see it. So the employer should have rules in place that limit the amount of sexually explicit material. Sadly, though, this isn't the case for everyone.

Whether you work in an office or a factory or a mechanic's shop, seductive material (coming from your boss, coworkers, or clients) can sometimes be a huge burden. And sometimes there's very little you can do about it.

But there are some things you *can* change. You can change your own personal workspace. You can eliminate anything that degrades women and defiles our sexuality. And you have to start there.

There are other places that are shared by coworkers, and often you can do something about that as well. Sometimes it might mean confronting someone about material they bring to work with them. Sometimes it might mean quietly 'sabotaging' unclean media. But before you launch into a full scale war against impurity at the workplace, you should take some time to choose your battles and consider the consequences.

I once worked at a car shop. Sex was probably one of the most popular subjects there among my coworkers (and even my superiors). Of course, most of them knew I was uncomfortable with it. Even though I was secretly addicted to pornography, I was still putting on the public mask of a pure Christian man. Once or twice I tried to urge them to keep certain comments to themselves—which made the subject that much more popular. In fact, most of the men there made it a point to bring up the subject whenever I was within hearing distance. You see—I would have heard much less of it if I had just ignored it and kept to my own work.

But there *were* some things I could control. For example, it was one of my duties to make sure the bathrooms were clean and in order. So whenever someone left a porn-mag in there, I simply threw it out with the trash. I didn't say anything about it. When asked, I simply shrugged my shoulders and went back to work. But they all knew not to leave their magazines in the bathroom—or any other area where I would be working.

There's also a thing you can do that you might have underestimated. Pray.

At another place I worked, one that was a bit more professional, there was a computer in the shop. Every now and then, my coworkers (all men) would stop at the computer and browse pornography. I was older by then and had learned a little more about dealing with people at work. So I usually just continued doing my own job without looking up. Sure, I could tell the boss. Maybe he would have done something about it. Or maybe he would have just given them a warning. Either way, whatever relationship I had with my coworkers (along with any influence I might have had) would have been demolished.

But I also prayed a lot. There was one particular time that two or three guys were surrounding the computer... all commenting on the bodies and helping the 'navigator' steer to this link or that one. I said a Hail Mary that they would stop. A few seconds later, the computer crashed. They weren't able to get it working again for a few days.

There was one individual at this place who gave me more trouble than the others. He loved to print pictures out and put them in places I would find them. He thought my embarrassment was one of the funniest parts of the day. This was during a 'clean' period when I was struggling with my purity and his jokes were a real source of temptation.

On my way to work one morning, I decided to pray an entire rosary just for him. Not for him to stop, not for him to get fired—just for his wellbeing.

The next week, he was promoted to a position outside of my department. I saw him only once a month after that, and he had moved on to other games.

So you see, if you're making an honest effort, God will help you along the way. It might not always be like a lightning bolt from the sky. God is subtle sometimes. But He'll give you what you need.

If it's possible for you to install filters on your work computer, do so. Sometimes a boss can be understanding about pornography addictions. I know of many men who have

114

confessed their addictions to their employers and were treated with kindness and understanding. If this is an option for you, great. But be aware that not every boss is going to see it that way. Admitting to misusing the computer at work can have serious consequences. Not that you would lie—but you're not obligated by God to tell everyone everything.

Purifying Your Sex Life

This section of the book is probably going to be the hardest one for you to accept. Because here is where a much harsher line is drawn. Here is where God is going to put you to the test: do you want to do it *His* way or not?

Abstaining

You've spent a fair amount of time filling your head with a fantasy. This doesn't just go away over night. Even after you've stopped looking at pornography, healthy sexual behavior isn't going to immediately follow. You have to actually repair what you've broken. And to do this, you're going to have to abstain for a while. Even if you're married. Even if your wife is completely willing to let by-gones be by-gones.

Most recovery programs agree that 60-90 days is a good start. During that time, you'll be helping yourself on several levels: physically, mentally, spiritually, and in your relationship with your wife.

Physically: In your 90 day abstinence period, you're going to re-master your sexual impulses. You'll starve your eyes, you'll starve your mind, and you'll starve your body. You'll gain the control you need to prove that your will is stronger than sex. This isn't like food and water, which you absolutely need in order to survive. You don't need sex at all, on a personal level. God handles the buildup of fluids, sperm, and hormones by giving us wet dreams. So it's silly to say that sex is a personal necessity. You need physical control of yourself, and this is the only way to get it.

Mentally: When you've gotten through this, you're going to feel so much strength. Mentally, it will help you for the rest of your life. Just knowing that you are in control again (with the help of God obviously) will give you the perseverance you'll need for years to come.

Spiritually: In the book of Samuel, the enemies of Israel stole the Arc of the Covenant. When they realized they had upset Israel's God, they not only returned the Ark, but they sent gold gifts as well—*guilt offerings*. To say, "I won't look at porn anymore," isn't good enough. That's something you should have been doing from the start. You need to sacrifice something. Sex, even though it isn't sinful *not* to sacrifice it, is a perfect offering to God for your sins. If you do this, God will help you.

In Your Relationship: Chances are, you'll *have* to abstain for a while anyway when you come clean with your wife. She's going to feel hurt and betrayed (rightly so), and probably isn't going to want to have sex for some time. Go with it and use that time to build strength. But during that time, you'll also be restructuring your perception of sex. You'll rediscover an amazing relationship... one you could have had all along but had traded in for your fantasies.

It's difficult to put into words the changes you'll go through. Think of back when you first began seeing your wife— back when you just couldn't wait to be with her. And finally, think of that time you first time you had sex with her—how fulfilling it was. You'll get some of that back, but it will be even more... because now you have so many life-events to look back on together.

Of course, sex won't always be so passionate, but you'll see the absolute detachment you've been experiencing disappear. And since you're also starving your eyes and mind, your wife (including the 'flaws' she's picked up from child bearing, child rearing, and age) will begin to look more attractive to you than she ever has before.

Again, there's no way to explain it in a way you can completely understand. It's something you have to experience in order to know. Remember how 'marriage jokes' sounded funny when you were young? And then, after getting married, they took on a certain irony—becoming even funnier than they were before? That's because when you were young, you could only be told about married life. Once you lived it though, you had a fresh understanding. A new perception.

It's the same with gaining a sacramental mastery of your sex life. When you come to the bed with your wife, and you both know that you are blameless before God, you're going to find new depths of intimacy that will nourish your relationship beyond your wildest dreams. And while you might miss the fantasies you had been holding onto, you'll find something much deeper to replace them with.

But this abstinence is part of that. You have to cleanse your system out, so that there's room for new growth. Clear the weeds, plant the flowers, and watch them bloom. It's hard work, but it's totally worth the effort.

Contraception

I have a feeling this next section is going to make me *very* unpopular.

Let's start with a simple, unbiased statement. An objective truth. Contraception is a mortal sin.

As Pope Pius XI says:

"In order that she [the Catholic Church] may preserve the chastity of the nuptial union from being defiled by this foul stain, she raises her voice in token of her divine ambassadorship and through our mouth proclaims anew: any use whatsoever of matrimony exercised in such a way that the act is deliberately frustrated in its natural power to generate life is an offense against the law of God and of

nature, and those who indulge in such are branded with the guilt of a grave sin."[20]

This is what the Church proclaimed since contraception's rise in popularity, it's what the Church proclaims now. This is not opinion. It's the law of God. And sadly, it's mostly ignored, even by Catholics.

Probably, you've heard a priest say that it's okay. On the pulpit or in the confessional you've heard it. You've probably also read false reports from the media that the Church is 'warming up' to it. But a priest can no more change Church teaching than the media can—and neither can a pope. The rule against contraception will never change. It can't change, because man cannot change God and it is God who has outlawed it.

I could write an entire book on why. I could fill page after page with the damage it does to relationships. But I won't, because you can already find such books and documents out there. Start with *Humanae Vitae* by Pope Paul VI.

The point I want to make here is that you are trying to purify your sex life. That means cleansing it of all sin. It means bringing God back into the marriage bed. In order to do that, you absolutely *must* devote your sex life to God. God, after all, created sex. He knew what He was doing... and He has good reasons for his rules.

But the most important reason for you, right now, is because contraception is a sin. If you sin in the bed, then you aren't exactly purifying sex, are you? You're still kicking God out. You're still trying to take up the reins and steer it yourself, aren't you?

This whole subject might create a huge stumbling block for you. Unlike the above section on abstaining, this is one of the necessities. You might be able to get by without abstaining for a long period of time (although I wouldn't suggest it). But you can't get through this if you're still ignoring God's commandments.

---

[20] Pope Pius XI, Casti Connubii, December 31, 1930, Section 4, Paragraph 4.

I won't say much more about the subject here. Either you believe me about this or you don't. If you have issues, then I would suggest using your period of abstinence (if you're going to go through one) to do some more reading on the subject. Pray about it at least. God will show you the way if you approach Him with an open heart.

But there's one problem—you're not the only one involved with this decision. Even if you come away thoroughly convinced that contraception is wrong, you still might not be able to convince your wife. She, after all, is the one who has to carry a child for 9 months.

So here is where your duties lie:

1. You do the research into this subject, and learn the facts as well as you can.
2. You pray about it, and accept God's guidance.
3. You approach your wife, telling her how you feel and the reasons for these feelings.
4. You provide her with any information you can.
5. You make it clear that you are against all contraception.
6. You refuse to practice it personally (as in—you will not wear a condom or 'get snipped.')
7. You allow her to make her own decision, praying that God will guide her as well.

After that, you can approach the marriage bed with a clear conscience. No, you don't have to abstain from sex if your wife insists on taking the pill or wearing a diaphragm. In fact, I wouldn't advise withholding sex as a means to change her mind. You've got enough working against you without building extra walls around yourself.

Now as for those who have already had an operation— you're not under an obligation to have it reversed. Go to confession and repent. Receive absolution. Get on with your life. If you're able to reverse it (meaning it won't put your body at risk and you have the financial means) then that's excellent. It will show a truly penitent heart. But you don't have to according to Church law.

Setting New Standards

What you do, how you think, and what you say are three connected things. So connected, in fact, that changing one will (in time) change the others. If you followed this book along, then you're making some very big changes in your life. You've starved your eyes and mind of sexual material—or anything at all that you'd be tempted to lust after. You've changed your lifestyle to match your new found purity. Probably, the language you use and the people you associate with are going to follow suit. You'll naturally find yourself *not* using certain language, and gravitating toward people who are like-minded.

But if it doesn't happen naturally, then it must happen deliberately. If not, then it could bring you back to trouble again. The sexual comments you make when you're with men, for example, will make you think more about sex. When you think about it more, it will tempt you (actually drive you) to act out. Then you're back to square one.

So in order to combat this, you're going to set new standards for yourself. You're going to make your outside appearance match the inner purity you're trying to obtain.

Dealing With Your Wife

This is one of the most important parts of recovery—how you deal with your wife. Whether you did it consciously or not, you've allowed yourself to turn your wife into an object. I've heard arguments from men who insist that they've never allowed their pornography addiction to interfere with their relationship— who say they've kept it out of their real bedroom.

I say that's bull. It's impossible not to let something like this creep into your relationship. It will do it in so many ways, and most of those ways you probably don't even recognize. Many of

120

them will disappear naturally, as I said before. But with a little effort on your part, they'll disappear faster and you and your wife will enjoy freedom in your relationship that you never even knew existed.

Let's start with the fact that your wife is precious. Oh, she can be mean sometimes. She can be a viper with her criticism or her demands. But she's still precious. She's precious, first of all, because she's a child of God. She's precious second of all because God gave her to you. He didn't give you the woman next door, or the receptionist at the office, or the fed-ex girl who visits the shop each day. He gave you your wife. And He gave you a very simple commandment: Love her as Jesus loves His church.

Love her more than you even love yourself. Jesus abandoned Himself for His church. He allowed Himself to be nailed to a cross. He faced toil and suffering. He did this all because he cherishes His church. In the same way, you must cherish your wife... more than anything on earth.

Generally, that doesn't mean filling yourself with luvy-duvy. In fact, it means loving your wife without the feelings. Yes, you should enjoy those emotional highs when they exist, but you must learn to behave the same way when they are absent. Your actions will fill the void that the emotions create when they temporarily disappear.

When you feel very close to your wife, you think nothing of jumping up and fetching her a drink simply because she says she's thirsty. You would draw her a picture, write her a poem, or buy her flowers just because you want to express the feelings you have for her. It's possible that you no longer have those strong feelings. But you still need to pretend that you do. Then, after months and months of cherishing her as though you'd never lost your emotional attachment to her, the feelings will begin to return. They won't be there always—they'll go up and down. But when they are present, you'll remember why you're working at it so hard.

Don't let a day go by without examining the way you're treating your wife. Ask yourself each night: *Am I cherishing God's gift?*

Don't play games with yourself either. Don't tell yourself that she'll be 'better off' if you deny her this or that. Obviously, we all have financial limits. We can't control those. You can't always buy her a new car because she wants one... or even flowers. But you have no limit on the love you can show her, except those you put on yourself.

There's one more thing that needs to be discussed concerning your wife. Let's say you've told her about your problem. After some cooling off time, she's accepted it and is doing her best to help you. She's put herself in a very vulnerable state now—not because she will accept your addiction, but because she wants to help you stop. Many men have used this circumstance to take advantage of their wives. The logic follows as such:

> *I need sexual fulfillment. I realize I can't get it from anyone but you. Because I have an addiction—because I'm not just sinful but actually sick—you should be there more often for me. Your body is my medication. The more sex I get from you, the less likely I am to fall.*

I've heard of men using this excuse to have sex more than once a day—and the wife, being so desperate to fix her marriage, gives freely.

If you take this approach, you will probably find your way back to pornography sooner or later. You must understand that your sexual impulses need to be reshaped and controlled—so that they don't control you. After all, what if your wife wasn't able to have sex with you. What if, heaven forbid, your wife died tomorrow? Would that give you an excuse to turn back to porn? No. The sexual relationship between a husband and wife is meant to be based on love, not on 'medicating.' If you turn it into medicating, you will never find true intimacy with your wife. And you'll miss out on the best part of the relationship.

Think of it this way: Sex should be a self giving act. Not one where you're taking. If you're doing it for your own satisfaction (without much thought into giving her what she needs) then you're not using sex the way God intended. It's not that you can't enjoy yourself. But if you're having sex TO enjoy yourself, then you're taking advantage of a situation.

Dealing With Family

Chances are, you won't tell everyone in your family (both immediate and extended family) about your addiction. If you have young children, they're obviously not old enough to comprehend it yet. And their innocence is valuable, so there's no reason to intrude on it just yet.

Older sons, however, might benefit from knowing about it. Not always, but sometimes. Whether or not you tell them will be between you, them, and God. There's not much advice anyone can give you on that, except to pray about it and do what you think the Holy Spirit is moving you to do.

But both your older and younger sons (and your daughters as well) can benefit right now from the example you set for them in the home. When they see you fast-forward commercials because of the scantily clad women on them, it sends them a very clear message about what it means to be a man. A man doesn't look at women as sex objects. A man turns his head. A man is strong against his own sexual desires. A real man is all about self control. When you send your kids these messages, it *will* have influence on them. Not right away, but over time. And there will come a time in their own lives when they will strive to be better (or in the case of your daughters, will expect better from the men they marry) because of your example.

Extended family can do a lot to help or hinder you. Especially if you're from a large Catholic family that stays somewhat connected as you grow older. I, for example, see my extended family on a regular basis. We talk a lot about the common things that people talk about—sports, politics, religion, cars, computers, and the latest DVDs. That last one, DVDs and movies, is a big one. Most of us appreciate a good sci-fi or action flick, and we're always ready to recommend one to each other.

But my brothers, knowing how much I am fighting to remain pure, understand that they can't recommend just *any* movie. As a matter of fact, they've gotten to the point where they even tell me what scenes I should not watch.

But you don't have to tell your family about your addiction in order to experience the same consideration. If you simply let it drop every now and then that you won't watch a certain movie "because it shows too much skin," they will eventually catch on. And more than likely, they'll begin to admire your purity.

Often, your brothers and father might be suffering from the same problem as you. Of course, that doesn't mean they're addicts. But every man has some degree of trouble turning away from sexually explicit material. If you do choose to tell them about your addiction, be prepared for a variety of reactions. Some might simply poo-poo the very idea that a man could be addicted to pornography. And that could be because they really don't struggle with it to the same degree that you do, or it could mean that they do and they're in denial. Either way, you can't force someone to see it the way you do. Others might understand completely, and even want to join you in your fight against it. But either way, don't depend on them for the support you need in this battle unless you know they completely understand the type of things you suffer from and understand how important it is that you break from pornography.

Aside from recommending movies, brothers have a way of conversing with each other. They're usually a bit more relaxed in their details about sex. You could say something in front of your brother that you certainly wouldn't say in front of a coworker or even one of your other friends. Because of this 'relaxation of social etiquette', it's important for you to try extra hard to clean up your language. No more degrading comments about women or their bodies. No more comments about the deterioration of your own wife's body. Obviously, two men who are close to each other will 'compare notes'. Discuss frequency or lack of frequency. Even technique. But it must not be discussed in a way that would degrade the act or the woman. Discuss sex from a Christian standard.

That doesn't mean you have to become the group censor and correct everyone else. But you can quietly drop out of a conversation when it turns in the wrong direction.

Dealing With Friends

You'll have to deal with your friends in about the same way as you deal with your brothers. Hold your tongue when the conversations turn sexual... unless it's more of a factual statement. Comments about a girl's butt or boobs are off limits. Talking about sex this way brings it to your mind more often. If you're in the habit of making such comments, then it will eventually change the way you think (or keep you from changing the way you think, depending on where you are in your recovery). And the way you think will soon change your actions. Presto— you're back on the computer looking up images and videos.

Friends will often pass around an 'interesting' pic on their mobile or even a picture from a magazine. Decline it politely. Let them know that this sort of thing doesn't really interest you. That it embarrasses you. That it even offends you. It doesn't have to be a fight or argument. If you know them well enough to call them friends, then a 'look' is all it will take to let them know you disapprove.

A real friend will not insist on showing you something you don't want to see. A real friend will not try to violate your sense of right and wrong. This is all the cliché stuff we heard from adults when we were in high-school. Most of us have found it to be true. If you haven't, then it's time to look for some new friends.

Now let's look at our growing list:

1. You are recognizing and admitting to the wrongs you commit... as soon as you realize it.
2. You are praying every day.
3. You are confessing your sins to a priest in a reasonable amount of time.

4. You are giving an accountability partner scheduled updates.
5. You are being honest and apologetic with your spouse, without burdening her with details.
6. You have specific responses to specific temptations, you know what they are, and you practice them constantly.
7. You don't think about your response—you just do it.
8. You keep destructive media out of your home and (as much as possible) out of your place of work.
9. You make every act of sex committed to God and your wife, allowing the possibility for children if it is God's will.
10. You cherish your wife and every night ask yourself if you've cherished her as Jesus cherishes His church.

Chapter 9 – Break All Triggers

When you deal with addiction, you deal with more than normal temptations. A girl with nice figure might be a temptation to you. It might even make you want to start that ritual you've grown so accustomed to. But because you've been using pornography and masturbation as a release—as a way to escape the pressures in life—then you're going to have certain 'triggers' that really have nothing to do with sex. This is where you're going to learn how to know, understand, avoid, and fight those triggers.

Differentiating Between Triggers And Temptations

A trigger is anything that begins the 'ritual' of looking at pornography or masturbating. A temptation (at least in the context of pornography addiction), which can be a trigger, is anything that excites you sexually.

For example, glancing across the street and seeing a jogger in tight shorts might create a temptation for you. You see more than you ought to see, and you *want* to see even more. It charges your sex drive. You might be tempted to get on the computer and look for other joggers. You might be tempted to go straight to the bathroom and masturbate. Or you might just be tempted to urge your wife to have sex. But your body's reaction to the woman is completely natural. It's not a 'learned behavior', and certainly isn't warped or perverted. All men have the reaction. All men must learn to deal with it. And we've discussed how to deal with it in previous chapters.

But a trigger isn't part of your natural sex drive. A trigger sets off a learned behavior pattern. Let's say you're having a bad day at work. When you get home, you immediately lock yourself in your bedroom or office and begin looking at pornography. This little ritual isn't based on natural sex drive. Stress at work doesn't charge a man sexually. For a lot of men, it does the opposite.

But for you, it starts off a chain reaction, which eventually plunges you into a fantasy world—one you've probably come to hate but can't seem to escape.

In order to quit pornography you have to learn to eliminate (or learn to deal with) temptations. But if the addiction has escalated very high, then you're also going to have to deal with your triggers. They can be harder to deal with than temptations, to a degree, because many of them are not 100% in your control. After all, you can't change the people around you and you can't always change your circumstances. But you can change your reaction to them. That's what you'll learn to do here.

Knowing Your Triggers

Triggers come in all forms. Most of them are stress points in your life. And if you were to look for a pattern, you'll probably find that your key triggers are stress points in your life that either you cannot change or that you would have a hard time changing.

Journals

One of the easiest ways to recognize your triggers is by journaling. When you keep a record of your mindset, emotional state, temptation level, and other significant things, you can look back at when you've fallen (or when you've been most tempted to fall) and you will see patterns.

You could go extensive, and treat it like a diary. Sometimes it's nice to bounce your thoughts, feelings, and ideas off of a sounding board. Some people do this by talking about it. Some by writing about it. Whatever the matter, men practically need a sounding board. For some reason, we get the funniest ideas, and they seem sound and logical until we hear or see them. Then we suddenly say, "Whoa—that would be a dumb thing to do!"

But you don't have to write that much if you're not comfortable writing. The real point is to document. A good format might be something like this:

128

- **Emotional State**: Just list the emotions you've felt throughout the day.
- **Work Day Rating**: Perhaps use a 1 – 10 rating system to describe how well your day went.
- **Home Day Rating**: The same as the work day rating system.
- **Relationship With Wife**: You could either use a simple rating system or describe any significant events (fights, long talks, sex, distant feelings, close feelings, etc.,)
- **Relationship With Kids**: Same as above.
- **Stress Rating**: How stressful your day was overall... and possibly what, if anything particular, caused your stress.
- **Temptation Level**: I would use a 1 – 10 scale, and then perhaps list things that made the day more tempting.
- **Triggers**: If you have a clear idea of what your triggers are already, then list them and how severe they were here.
- **Failures**: List the ways you've fallen and how hard (for example, "looked at porn for 2 hours")
- **Victories**: Life isn't always about struggles and failures. It's important to remind yourself of the good things you've done and the battles you've won.

You could add or take away from this list. The journal is for you, as an aid to finding out what is causing you to jump to destructive behaviors. You'll probably find out that it will help you in more areas than your sexual addiction. It will help you see patterns with anger issues, chemical abuse, and plenty of other things.

Once you've been journaling for several months, go back and start to look for patterns. If you've been using a numeral rating system, you could make a line graph of your stress levels, failures, and temptation levels. You'd most likely see that they correlate.

You don't have to find a way to cut the stress out of your life. You just have to figure out what stresses you the most, and then find a different way to react to the stress.

Emotional States

The reason many men get sucked into the habit of looking at pornography is because it is a form of escapism. Whether you're worried about bills, stressed out because of your job, depressed because of your relationship with your wife, or just frustrated with your kids, pornography offers a brief 'zone-out time'... or a not so brief one. Many men can disappear into the profane pictures for hours at a time, not once thinking about their problems. But as you've already seen, this actually makes the problems worse... and causes additional problems as well.

So even without keeping an actual journal, you probably have a good idea of what your triggers are. If you can't pinpoint specific circumstances (like after you see the energy bill or just after a fight with your wife), you can at least pay attention to certain states that seem to drive you to pornography.

Depression is one of the most common. And if you've been medicating your depression for a long time (like say, years) then you might very well have a chronic depression problem. But depression isn't always the easiest thing to spot—especially for men. I, for example, didn't always experience the sadness that most people associate with the word depression. Sometimes I didn't feel sad at all, even though I was in a *deep* state of depression—nearly suicidal in fact. But in my mind, I thought, "I'm not sad—I must not be depressed." Here are some of the signs to look for to see if you're depressed:

- **Isolation:** Depression often makes you want to shut everything and everyone out. This was obviously what you were doing when you were looking at pornography; but even if you successfully quit, you might find yourself replacing the pornography and masturbation with

130

something else. Video games, long periods of reading by yourself, watching television or listening to music by yourself (especially depressing movies or music), and just spending hours alone are all ways you might isolate yourself from the rest of the world—which is a clear indication of chronic depression.

- **Restlessness:** If you're a family man, there's probably a list of at least 60 different things you could be doing at any given time. And yet, you walk from room to room, trying to find something to do. This is restlessness. It was one of my biggest symptoms during my depression. Before my recovery began, it almost always led to me being on the computer looking at pornography.

- **Oversleeping:** Sleep, like pornography, is a way of escaping our problems. You should be getting 6-7 hours a night. If you find yourself sleepy after that, then you could very well be dealing with depression. Of course tiredness could be caused by many other things as well, like sleep apnea, malnutrition, or a host of other health issues. Talk to your doctor about it if this is becoming a problem for you.

- **Over or Under Working:** Some guys feel depression and deal with it by working long hours. Other guys feel depressed and suddenly feel incapable of doing their share of work, whether it's at home or in the office. Too much in either direction is harmful. It can interfere with your relationships with friends, family, and God.

- **Overreacting:** Anger issues are a big indication of depression. You're floating through your day when you hit just a tiny speed bump (like one of the kids spilling a drink). Suddenly, you're acting as if the world is about to end—whether that means screaming and yelling or hurting someone.

Panic or anxiety attacks are other common triggers. Sometimes they can either creep up out of nowhere. Sometimes they can follow a clear pattern and have association with events and/or circumstances. They're always frightening.

Panic attacks, like depression, might seem like something that would be very apparent and recognizable. But, like depression, that's not always the case. I used to deliver pizzas for a local company in Cincinnati. One night, I got mugged. I wasn't hurt, and after filling out the police reports, I thought it was over—I'd just resume my life again. The next evening, just at dusk as things got darker, I went out on a delivery. I wasn't scared. I felt no fear whatsoever. But suddenly my heart was pounding as if I'd just run a marathon. I had a weird sensation in my belly— the sinking feeling you get on a rollercoaster. All the physical signs of fear were there, *but I wasn't scared!* Finally I realized, "This is a panic attack—that's what they mean when they talk about panic attacks."

Panic and anxiety attacks can be a huge trigger for men. Pornography gives them a nice little world where anything can happen... where even the laws of God are bent for them. Where there are no bill collectors or responsibilities. No one insults them or abuses them.

But don't fool yourself into thinking it will help the situation. Like with depression, pornography will only make the over-all problem worse. The longer you put off dealing with severe emotional states, the more problematic they will become.

Changing Your Responses

Panic, depression, and other emotional problems are often out of our control—as are many triggers. They are brought on by outside circumstances and events. But we *can* control how we deal with it. We can respond to our triggers by plopping down in front of the computer and looking at pornography... or by finding

132

a more constructive response. One that will both help the problems that cause our triggers and help us in our overall recovery.

There are two different strategies you might want to consider. One would be to avoid the trigger (the emotional state that a specific thing causes) altogether. The other would be to respond differently to the trigger.

Avoiding The Trigger

This is another area where journals would be very helpful. Mostly because we're usually not clear headed enough to consider our options and see the consequences *while* we're struggling with a trigger.

For example, let's say one of your triggers is when your wife insults you. She might start by saying you're not earning enough money for the family or that you're letting the house maintenance slide. You defend yourself, complaining about her spending habits. She defends herself by attacking *your* spending habits. Eventually, both of you are shouting out insults that have nothing to do with the original subject. And soon your masculinity is under attack (a big trigger for *many* men). It plunges you into a deep depression, and you find yourself looking for an escape.

At one point in the process, you took a morally wrong turn. Perhaps it was the first insult you dealt. Perhaps it was the first time you began to raise your voice. Or maybe it was the general attitude you had during the whole conversation. That's something you'd have to examine later—after your anger is gone and after you've gotten over the depression it might have set off.

But long before the morally wrong turn, you took another wrong turn. Not one that was sinful, necessarily, but one that turned the conversation into an argument. Probably, it was the point at which you responded to her initial complaint. The very first words out of your mouth.

Put the conversation in your journal and look back on it the next day in the aftermath. When you're rational, think about how the conversation went and how you could have kept it from becoming a fight. Remember now, that **your objective is not to convince her of anything**. Your objective is to keep it from becoming a fight—thus killing the trigger before it even exists.

My friends and I have a phrase that we use. We say our wives are *"sending us to Fedex."* This comes from a commercial Fedex had. A caveman ties a parcel to the leg of a pterodactyl. As it flies off, another dinosaur jumps up and kills it. The caveman goes to the boss caveman and says the package didn't make it. The boss caveman fires him for not using Fedex, even though Fedex doesn't exist yet. Ever since that commercial, every time our wives want the impossible (or are angry at us for something way beyond our control) we say we're *going to Fedex.*

Going to Fedex can be a trigger in and of itself. But the fights that ensue because of being sent to Fedex can be even worse. For example, if your income is well out of your control (as it is for many men) you will feel pressure. If your wife is expecting you to do something about it, and you're completely unable to, the fights will put even more pressure on you.

This is why I say that your objective (when you plan your next 'encounter') is not to convince your wife (or anyone else) of anything. You must discern between what's going to end the conversation amicably and what's going to cause more problems—whether the conversation is between you and your wife or you and your boss (most men agree that both conversations are the same).

For example, the conversation mentioned earlier could have gone like this:

> HER – I'm tired of this s$$t! You need to get a second job. We can't survive on your income.

> YOU (with a wide goofy grin) – I was gonna sell you to my cousin, and then use the money to pay off the mortgage. You're good with that, right?

HER – I'm serious—you need to do something. You're
    being lazy.
YOU (still with a smile) – Yeah. Ain't it weird how you still
    love me though?
HER (walking off in a mixed state of emotions, half smiling
    & half frowning) – Whatever.

In the conversation above, you didn't agree or disagree with her complaint. You simply changed the subject. It's much easier to think of a response like this after-the-fact. So do it after-the-fact, and remember your plans the next time the subject comes up. Even highlight the event in your journal, and right next to it explain how you'll react differently next time to keep it from becoming a trigger.

You can't necessarily avoid all subjects by joking. But you *can* at least postpone them. You can agree with her to talk about it at a certain time later. This will help you to prepare for the conversation and set some rules for yourself. That way, the conversation won't spin out of control quite as quickly.

What you're trying to avoid is the reactionary responses that eventually turn into triggers. In the example above, not a whole lot can be solved by going through your life's income and expenses at that exact time. In fact, *most* arguments between spouses over finances are spur of the moment and they very rarely solve anything. They usually begin as griping. Always remember that griping doesn't *have* to turn into a discussion. If your wife wants to gripe about lack of money (or your lack of hygiene or pretty much anything at all) then let her. It's not hurting you. If it does need to be discussed seriously, you can schedule a time to discuss it.

Respond To The Trigger

Of course, you can't always completely avoid a trigger. Bills and financial situations often become triggers. As do relationships at work, stressful events, and sometimes even loneliness. The most you can do is to change the way you react to the triggers.

This is one area where a hobby can become a real life-saver. Remember our axioms at the beginning of this book? Axiom #4 was that men are obsessive. We have a tendency to completely submerge our minds into things. I knew a guy who decided he wanted to try gardening one summer. Two years later, his entire back yard was divided up into plots, each having a different kind of veggie or flower. The next year, he had converted a room in his house into a growing room, where he raised plants from seed before putting them in the yard. Maybe not all men are quite that bad, but we all have a tendency to dive into things and organize the rest of our lives around such hobbies.

Use this to your advantage. Turn your obsession with sex into an obsession with something harmless (if not productive).

Before we continue, I just want to clarify one thing: video gaming is not a hobby. A hobby either produces something or develops a specific, productive skill or talent. Video gaming is another means of escape, and, like pornography, is usually destructive.

If you don't have a hobby, it might be time to pick one. Every boy should have a pet dog, every girl should have a favorite doll, every man should have a hobby.

Your hobby doesn't necessarily have to reflect one of your natural talents. It would be more fulfilling if it did, but it doesn't have to. I once went through a six month phase of learning to play the trumpet (my wife had picked up a used one at Goodwill for $20). I knew from the start that I'm terrible with music. I knew that I would never be able to play by ear or even be able to play freestyle. But by golly, I had decided I would learn at least six songs on that horn, and I stuck with it until I had learned six songs. I used free instructions I had found online. It took me almost a week of practice before I was able to play a single note (you have to build up the muscles in your lips). I bothered my kids, my wife, and the dog with my constant tooting (most of it being *waaayyy* off-key). But it helped me forget about some of the stress in my life and therefore improved the lives of everyone in the household.

The key here is having something you can turn to when you begin to feel panic or depression. It's a distraction, so to speak. When you were learning to distract your attention away from the bodies of women, I had given you a list of other things to focus on. This is the same concept, only the distractions are for longer periods—enough to even change your moods.

As I was learning to play the trumpet, I was in the middle of a particularly long clean period. But it was a very stressful time in my life financially. I would get a bill in the mail or get a call from a collector, and suddenly find myself in an extreme state of panic... which was a huge trigger that constantly pulled me in the direction of pornography. I allowed myself to feel that way for a half hour (some amount of stress is healthy), decided what action (if any) I would take to help the situation, and then refuse to think about it any further for that day. I would pull out that horn and blow on it for about ten minutes. Usually, I was struggling with a particular note or set of notes. And even after I put the trumpet down, I would continue thinking about it, wondering why I couldn't hit a certain note or memorize a set. My mind would stay with that trumpet for a good long time.

For some reason, the motivation I had for the trumpet would spill over into other areas in my life. As if overcoming a problem with music made it possible to overcome a problem with the bills. No—trumpet playing didn't pay the mortgage. But sitting and worrying about the mortgage wouldn't pay it either. So once I had decided on what my next move was (concerning bills or relationships or work or anything at all), then there was no need to keep thinking about it anyway. I would think about something more manageable—like the trumpet.

That's how a hobby will help you. By giving your mind an inconsequential distraction. By giving you a healthy response to triggers.

Remember in the beginning I had mentioned that some men will stick to the same hobby for years and years, while others jump from one to another. I myself am a jumper. I also spent most of my life below poverty level. The point is, you don't have to have money to start a hobby, so don't make the excuse, "I want to do this, but I have to save up enough money to start." Below, I've listed a number of my own personal hobbies, along with how I started them with little or no money.

- **Music:** As mentioned in my earlier example, you can usually find an instrument relatively cheap at a second hand store. My wife came home with an accordion once. It cost only $5 and YouTube has hundreds of how-to videos. I once borrowed a banjo from an uncle, and learned to play that over a period of several years. But everything I've learned was just a matter of memorizing the finger movements. And all of the instructions were beginner's courses that I found free online or books borrowed from the library. Mouth harps and harmonicas are also good choices because you can carry them around in your pocket and practice any time you want.

- **Star Gazing:** Telescopes can cost thousands of dollars. The cheap ones you find in toy stores aren't even worth bothering with. But you can find a decent one here and there for less than $20 in various second-hand stores. Besides, you don't necessarily need a telescope to star gaze. Until you have one, you can study the free star charts found online and learn to spot various stars, planets, and constellations by memory. My boys and I would do this for an hour or so each clear night. It gave me a distraction as well as something the boys and I could do together.

- **Beads & Jewelry:** Okay—it's not the most masculine thing in the world. But it's something you can do with your hands. My wife and I made rosaries—making them for ourselves and eventually for gifts. You can find practice

138

materials pretty cheap. Just use plastic beads and crosses until you have enough to invest in something better. You can also buy old, cheap jewelry from second hand stores and scavenge the beads from them to make your own designs.

- **Writing:** It takes very little to start a hobby like writing. Just a pen and a few sheets of paper. If you think you have something, you can invest in a computer later. But even then, you might find that you enjoy writing your rough drafts by hand anyway.

- **Wood Working:** One day I got it in my head that my kids needed some dominoes. Instead of buying dominoes, I borrowed a friend's cross-cut saw, bought three 2X4's, and made a ton of over-sized dominoes. That, of course, brought on a different obsession with domino tracks. But it also made me realize how easy it is to make things on my own. I started picking up small shelves and wooded furniture from garage sales (rarely spending more than a buck at a time), disassembling the wooden parts, and reusing the wood to make something completely different. I got hours of work, a few bucks spent, and a few neat conversational pieces to have around the house.

- **Sewing:** My daughter told me she needed a pair of jean shorts. I told her to bring me a pair of jeans she didn't want anymore, and I cut the legs off and sewed on some hems (I had to look up how to sew online). Then I picked up some more jeans at Goodwill, and found ways to make the hems better. I also found out I could turn them into skirts. Then I realized I could also make matching purses. This phase didn't last very long, but I have a few interesting pieces to show for it.

- **Cooking:** Hey, you have to eat anyway. Why not get into it? I started with recipes I looked up in old cook-books or online. As I learned more what the various spices do, I found myself parting from the recipes and trying new things on my own. Some of them turned out okay, most of them were disastrous. It gave the family a chance to try new foods, and it gave me something to think about during the day. In fact, I found myself looking forward to dinner, just so I could try out one thing or another and see what everyone thought.

Again, you don't necessarily have to have a talent in order to start a hobby. In most of the hobbies listed above, I had very little or no talent at all. You just have to be committed to trying it for a certain amount of time. Set some goals for yourself and see what happens.

Breaking Behavior Patterns

A hobby is only one way to respond to a trigger. There are many different ways, and you can use any way you want. The point is to break the behavior pattern that used to lead you to pornography. Replace the destructive behavior (looking at porn or masturbating) with something more Christ-like.

In my own recovery, I was subject to very deep depression. So deep that I almost felt I had been chained. I knew that I should get up and do something with myself. I knew sitting around and thinking about problems wasn't going to solve anything. But I felt completely powerless. I *wanted* to get up and work on one of the many hobbies I had started, but I just *couldn't*.

NOTE: These feelings are very common during the 3rd stage of purity. It's during this time that you begin to feel like saying, "So what? So I've stayed off pornography for X months. My life's no better. Why bother?"

This is just after the honeymoon stage. You've forgotten the pain you felt when you were trying to escape pornography. And now, the feeling of joy and freedom are slowly fading.

This is a very critical time. A time in which your triggers will drive you to pornography *more* than temptation will. It's very important that you find a way to deal with your triggers. If not, you'll find yourself back to day one. You must find a way to get back into the mundane struggles in life without allowing pornography to creep back in.

Of course, during such times before my recovery, I would just wait around for some alone time so that I could hop on the internet and plunge into my fantasy world. But now I couldn't do that. So I knew that I had to find a different way to deal with depression, repeat those actions every time I felt depressed, and allow this to become a pattern—a learned behavior that would lift me up instead of bringing me down.

I decided to start with a very simple physical activity. Something I could do with my hands, but not actually think about it. For me, it was cleaning. Not for long, and no huge projects. I might force myself to sweep a floor, do a pan full of dishes, or fold half a load of laundry. The point was to create the first step in a new pattern. You're not finished with that step—it's not going to break your trigger. It's just going to get you started.

After cleaning for a short time, I would switch to something a little more relaxing—but still physical. I was partial to horse shoes (I had some pits in my backyard). If I couldn't do that, I might toss football with my son. Or I might just play 'tickle monster' with my kids.

Finally, I would either jump into one of my hobbies or find something else that was more mental than physical. A lot of times I would help my kids with their homework. That in itself was a mental challenge—especially for my teenager who needed help with algebra. It was during my worse struggle that I started writing this very book.

You don't have to do it this way exactly. Think for a while about how you can create your own pattern. Something you'll be able to do every time these triggers creep up on you. As you learn this behavior pattern (as it becomes part of your routine) you'll find yourself automatically reacting to triggers in a positive way. It will dampen the temptation while improving your overall life.

It's a win-win.

Getting Counseling

I'm not much of one to sit around and cry about my problems (past or present)... especially if I have to pay someone to listen to me. Most therapists and counselors focus on people's pasts, whereas I would rather see someone fix the present.

But I'm also not one to go meddling in a field I know nothing about. Did I go to counseling during my recovery? Yes I did. Did it help? Yes. Was it necessary? I don't know. But what I do know is that my specific counselor did not urge me to drone on and on about childhood traumas. He was direct in telling me where I was going wrong and how to fix it. And much of what he told me is in this book.

But there are those out there who have some very distinct problems that need to be worked out in order to truly recover. Sometimes depression or anxiety needs to be dealt with by a professional who can find the source of emotional problems and help overcome it.

There's also a certain amount of escalation that may have occurred—the kind that will require special help. If you've found yourself looking at child pornography, having same sex attractions, or some other escalation that isn't dealt with in this book, then you should seek help.

But counselors cost money, and not everyone has it. Insurance will often pay a certain amount of counseling services. If you don't have insurance, or insurance won't pay for it, you might look into some kind of religious social services in your area... whether it's Catholic or not. The Catholic Social Services in my area is pretty good and they provide financial aid for individuals and families who need counseling but can't afford it. If you don't have such a service in your area, you might just start calling some of the churches around you and see if they can refer you to a Christian counselor who will see someone on a discounted rate.

Calling A Partner

Remember at the end of Chapter 2, I said that you should be forming alliances in a 12 step program? This is why. There are going to be times you just can't force yourself away from a trigger. Times that you feel you're no longer in control. Your feet, your hands, and even your mind are all moving you toward one end. You know what that end is. You don't want to go there. But you find yourself going anyway.

It takes only a few seconds to pull your phone out and speed dial one of your allied troops. If that soldier is busy or doesn't answer, it takes a few more seconds to call the next one on your list. Those few seconds can mean the difference between failure and victory.

Will it feel weird calling an accountability partner (or mentor or whoever you can reach from your support group)? Yes it will—the first few times anyway. But your partners have probably been in your shoes before. They know how it feels to struggle the way you are. And sometimes just a few words of encouragement can lift you out of that darkness. It can put you on your feet again and make you feel like, "Yes—this is manageable. I can do this. I can be the man God wants me to be."

Not convinced? Think about this: Did Jesus carry His cross all by Himself?

No. Jesus had help. Jesus needed help. Jesus' body would not have gotten that cross up the steep hill if someone hadn't helped Him. For Him, this was a choice. He could have miraculously had everything levitate and just float to Calvary. But

He didn't do it that way. He showed His need for help, and accepted the help given to Him.

You have a cross to bear. A heavy one. You're no better than Jesus... and unlike Jesus, you can't choose whether to do it alone or accept help. If you want to get that cross to Calvary, then you *have* to accept help.

Your partners are your Simons. They will help you carry the load when your will is weak. They'll pick you up before you hit the ground. But they can't help you if you don't call. You have to be the one to initiate contact and ask for help.

In the middle of a workday, call them. In the middle of the night, call them. You might have to give them a few minutes to wake up, get to a place they can talk, or to call you back. But if you have an accountability partner, it's because he wants to help. He will help. Just make the call.

Now for our list:

1. You are praying every day.
2. You are confessing your sins to a priest in a reasonable amount of time.
3. You are giving an accountability partner scheduled updates.
4. You are being honest and apologetic with your spouse, without burdening her with details.
5. You have specific responses to specific temptations, you know what they are, and you practice them constantly.
6. You don't think about your response—you just do it.
7. You keep destructive media out of your home and (as much as possible) out of your place of work.
8. You make every act of sex committed to God and your wife, allowing the possibility for children if it is God's will.
9. You cherish your wife and every night ask yourself if you've cherished her as Jesus cherishes His church.

144

10. You know your triggers and have prepared responses to them.
11. You keep a list of friends to call... and use them as often as necessary.

Chapter 10 – Include God

For several years, I spent a lot of time listening to a great preacher on Catholic radio. He was a priest who makes you excited about being Catholic. As did many of his listeners, I learned a lot from him. His testimony was one of those 180 stories, where he had been addicted to drugs, women, and money. He spiraled down and hit rock bottom, and only God could lift him up again. Then he had gone through many struggles, but he eventually became a priest. His story was inspiring and motivational... and he was a great speaker.

And then came the big news—he was being accused of sexting, soliciting prostitutes, alcohol abuse, drug abuse, and breaking his vow of poverty. I thought, "No way. Not this guy. He's doing God's work. And he does it so well."

I continued this denial for a while, until the order he belonged to sent out a press release stating that it looked like most of the accusations were true. He had fallen.

If you've listened to Catholic radio much (or if you've watched EWTN very often) then you know who I'm talking about. It sent my mind into complete disorder.

Here was a man trying to bring people closer to God. I can understand that no one is impervious to the attacks of Satan. I can understand that we all have to stand strong. But really— doesn't God have some kind of special help for those who are out there battling for Him?

Of course what this really brought to mind was the fact that *I* could fall just as easily. If this guy was susceptible, then how much more likely am I to sink back into my old habits and sins? It really scared the hell out of me.

After a lot of thinking, reading, praying, and researching, I came to the conclusion that there's only one answer to all of this. There's only one way to stay ahead of the Devil and all his tricks. There's only one way to make a long-term recovery and never turn back to a sinful life. And that is to form a complete alliance with God. One that covers every corner. One that won't let any sins slip in unexpectedly.

So far, we've been working on pornography addiction. How to allow God to change the way you think about sex, about women, and about your own masculinity. And maybe you thought that you would be able to cure your sexual addiction but keep the rest of your life set up the way it always had been. But God doesn't just want this one tiny corner of your life. God wants all of you. He made you with a special purpose in mind, and you'll have to completely surrender to his will before you can fulfill that purpose.

Accepting Forgiveness

The first step to allowing God to work in your life is understanding that you've been forgiven. Knowing you've been forgiven. Accepting God's mercy and allowing His blood to wash away your sins. Jesus carried a heavy cross—paid a heavy price—for your sins. Your sins *cannot* outweigh His sacrifice. If you think your sins are greater than God's mercy, then you are belittling His sacrifice.

Does that mean you should look forward in life and never think about the terrible things you've done? Never ponder the problems you've caused or allow yourself to feel the shame that pornography brought upon you? Certainly not. We must, from time to time, reflect on our sins of the past. To meditate on the many times we've let God down and committed ourselves to the evil one.

But these reflections should lift us up, not bring us down. We look at our past in the context of how great God is—how He can change our lives and touch our souls.

This is difficult to do if you've been standing in the darkness for a long time. Even if it's not on a conscious level, you've slipped into the habit of thinking of yourself as displeasing to God. On the other hand, your attitude on the surface may have been ignoring your problems and allowing yourself to think that your actions didn't matter all that much. You may have been too presumptuous of God's mercy on the outside, but in denial of God's forgiveness on the inside. There's a precarious line between presumption and despair... one we have to walk carefully.

Think about the following verses from Psalms:

The Lord ruleth me: and I shall want nothing.

He hath set me in a place of pasture. He hath brought me up, on the water of refreshment:

He hath converted my soul. He hath led me on the paths of justice, for his own name's sake.

For though I should walk in the midst of the shadow of death, I will fear no evils, for thou art with me. Thy rod and thy staff, they have comforted me.

Thou hast prepared a table before me against them that afflict me. Thou hast anointed my head with oil; and my chalice which inebreateth me, how goodly is it!

And thy mercy will follow me all the days of my life. And that I may dwell in the house of the Lord unto length of days.[21]

This Psalm, as popular as it is, is often looked at as a way to get through trouble and hardship. A source of inspiration to help a man skip through life without having to worry about the dangers of this world. Many fail to see the real meaning behind it—MERCY. And mercy only happens *after* repentance.

You've been lifted now. You've seen the errors of your ways, and strive hard to avoid them. You've decided to turn your life around—to be a servant of God and to run from the devil's

---

[21] Psalms 23

many temptations. You've begun building your strength, so that you can battle all evil. You've become a man again. You've lurked in the "shadow of death" for so long, succumbing to every temptation, but now God has lifted you and you've accepted His salvation.

Taste the cool water of refreshment now. Understand that the sins of the past cannot harm your soul. You might, in a worldly sense, have to pay for what you've done. You might have damaged some things and now have to repair them. But those evils (the ones creeping in the shadows) cannot reach you through God's mercy. You are clean now. Enjoy the comfort of God's *rod* and *staff*—the tools God uses to keep you from straying.

Moving Beyond Pornography

I'm sure you've heard the phrase, "Every man needs a vice." Well I can say without a doubt that this is a lie. It's one men tell themselves when they don't want to let go of something. It's true that every man has a weakness—something he's more or less prone to. But a vice is when we allow our weaknesses to overcome our will. For example, when we allowed pornography to keep us chained and bound to a life of sin. You're working on that vice now, and hopefully have made great strides in the way of purity.

But what other weaknesses do you have? Have any of them become vices? Do you drink too much? How about drugs? Do you have trouble controlling your anger? Have you been gambling? Do you tend to spend too much money on worldly goods? Do you spend too much time watching television or playing video games? Do you eat the wrong foods, only to satisfy your tastes instead of nourishing your body?

All of these (along with hundreds more) are things that Satan can use to get his foot back into your life. No, playing too many video games or eating too many donuts might not be as bad as spending hours watching porn videos. But sin, like holiness, spreads.

Remember what Jesus said:

He that is not with me, is against me: and he that gathereth not with me, scattereth.[22]

Either you are totally on God's side, and you continuously find ways to become more holy, or you will fall—are already falling, in fact. God does not accept a middle ground. And I hate to tell you this, but neither does Satan. The only difference is, God is up front about what He expects. He tells us from the very start that He wants us to serve him exclusively. Satan, on the other hand, will try to convince you that you don't have to turn over everything—that you can reserve some space for yourself without losing your salvation. It's a lie. Believe me, it's a lie. If you give audience to Satan, even a small amount, he will swallow you whole.

There were times throughout my life that I desired to grow in holiness. Even during the times I was so heavily dependent on pornography. But the pornography kept me so overwhelmed with grief and shame, I thought it would be impossible to grow anywhere else. For example, I wanted to quit drinking excessively (something that was steadily developing into a problem). But then I would say to myself, "Let's just work on the pornography first... then, when I'm better from that, I can think about alcohol."

This is a nice, easy way of saying, "Don't work on anything at all." Not that I thought of it that way, but I eventually realized that you can (and sometimes must) work on several problems at a time. Drinking, for instance, was making it much hard to give up pornography. And when I stopped drinking, it made it that much easier to stop looking at porn. One habit supports another. Quitting one will kill that support.

---

[22] Matthew 12:30

Overcoming Other Habits And Problems

Many of the habitual sins can be overcome using the same tactics you used against pornography. It's a matter of changing your response to temptations and (if it's become an addiction) triggers. You need a physical response—one you can decide on beforehand and act on later.

Anger

Many men struggling with a pornography addiction also have anger management issues. Especially when dealing with their families. As a matter of fact, a lot of women who have reconciled with husbands struggling with pornography say that they suffered more from the coldness, distance, and anger of their husbands than from the hurt and betrayal.

And like pornography addiction, overcoming anger will involve some life changes. You must reestablish, in your daily routines, a way looking at and reacting to the world... especially when it involves your wife and children. Start by focusing your attention on the small conversations you have with them. Show more interest in their lives—even if you don't always feel interested. When your wife or children tell you a story they think is funny, laugh with them—even if you aren't all that much amused. When you come home from work, rekindle the love by seeking out each member of your family and greeting them as if you've missed them throughout the day—even if you didn't.

Unfortunately, anger doesn't always announce itself quite as much as lust does. It can come on unexpectedly and you can find yourself involved in a passionate tantrum before you're even aware that you are getting out of control. The key to overcoming the problem lies is telling yourself to remain calm each and every time you begin a conversation. When a child runs up to you to report a spilled drink, a fight with a sibling, or a request (whether it's to go somewhere or to watch a television show) prepare for the conversation before you reply. Tell yourself that, no matter what, you're going to remain in control.

This is especially important when you have to discipline a child. My own anger issues had gotten so out of hand that I had to enforce a strict 'no physical contact' policy on myself when it came to disciplining my children. Unless I had to physically remove a child from danger, I wouldn't allow myself to touch them until five minutes after the 'infraction.' I had to fight hard to resist the habitual responses I had learned—namely that of giving immediate spankings when my children misbehaved. Of course, when they saw I was taking a new approach, they immediately tried to test it—to push me to my limits. But I hung tight, and we now all have a better relationship.

Drinking / Drugs

As you root out the lust in your life, your body will look for something to replace it. If you drink occasionally, you'll probably feel the urge to do it more frequently. And if you have any kind of drug habit, then the problem will only get worse. My suggestion: be proactive and address chemical habits now.

It might be a good idea to stop drinking altogether (even the one or two beers you have at dinner time) as you dry out sexually. If you find that you can't stop drinking or if you already recognize a chemical dependency, then get help now. Fortunately, there are already dozens of support groups for drug addictions—finding one near you shouldn't be difficult. One of the reasons I recommend Celebrate Recovery, is because they deal with multiple habitual sins. You can work on your chemical dependencies *while* you get support for your pornography struggle.

Television / Video Games

If you spent a lot of time looking at pornography, you'll naturally find yourself with a lot of 'free time' when you quit. One of the easiest things to do is to fill that time with television (even if it's "quality Catholic programming") and/or video games. But this is only substituting. You had once medicated yourself with pornography, now you're escaping the same problems with other forms of electronic entertainment.

You can set time limits on yourself and follow them strictly. If you find yourself breaking those time limits, then that should tell you that you have a problem with it. You need to break away from it entirely. Dry out for a while. Find something else (something more productive) to fill your time.

Spending Time With God

In the modern Catholic culture, we have a certain way of looking at prayer. We say novenas. We ask for God to accomplish this or that. We pray for guidance and counsel. We pray that our mortgage can be paid. We pray that we can find the car keys. We pray for just about everything.

But sometimes, we forget to just pray—for nothing specific.

What I mean is, it's easy as a Catholic to look at prayer as a request line. Sometimes even as a vending machine—where we insert a certain number of prayers and expect to receive a certain amount of favor. Some people refer to this as "push-button prayer."

It's true that God wants us to come to Him with all of our troubles. To ask Him for favors and to realize in our hearts that He is the source of all of our strength. But at the same time, we must realize that prayer is not like a magic spell. We can't force God's hand in anything. We can only ask, and then allow God to work as He wills.

And sometimes, we have to realize that prayer is not always about communication. But it is always about communion—about *being* with God. Open to Him and in humble union. Prayer is a state—not just an action.

Spreading God

Jesus told us:

You are the light of the world. A city seated on a mountain cannot be hid.

Neither do men light a candle and put it under a bushel, but upon a candlestick, that it may shine to all that are in the house.

So let your light shine before men, that they may see your good works, and glorify your Father who is in heaven.[23]

Now that you've killed the darkness in your life, now that you've let in the light, do you really think you should contain it? Do you really think you'll be *able* to contain it?

If you've been able to turn away from pornography, then God is at work in your life. And your responsibility, as the recipient of God's grace, is to allow God to work *through* you, not just *on* you.

You might have heard this saying before: Preach the Gospel, and if necessary use words. Sadly, many men use it to justify never talking about God. People often attribute it to St. Francis of Assisi. Judging from his life and his own actions, he probably never said it. St. Francis, as with all the saints, was pretty vigilant about openly proclaiming the Word of God. Not just in action, but in words as well.

It's true that there are times and places that are inappropriate for evangelization. And during those times, you should find other ways to distinguish yourself as a Christian. At work, for example, you might not be able to tell your coworkers about Jesus' sacrifice on the cross. But you can be a loyal, honest, and hard worker—showing them you have something inside you (the burning passion for Christ) that makes you different from other people. A simple rosary hanging in your cubicle/office/workshop/corner/car identifies you as a Catholic, so that they know exactly what it is that drives you. And you can

---

[23] Matthew 5:14-16

drop hints here and there. For example, when a coworker dumps on you about his or her troubles, you can say, "I'll pray for you." instead of "That really bites, I hope things get better."

The point is, even if you can't get on a soap box, you can still preach the Gospel. You can still evangelize. And this is something God *expects* you to do.

Pretend, for a second, that you're a great musician. You and your band put together a song (or even a whole album), record it, and make a few copies to give to people. Everyone who listens to it absolutely loves it. Your closest friends and family members tell you it's the best they've ever heard. In fact, you often find them listening to your music, even when they don't know you're there. But then not one of them shares the songs with their other friends... or even listens to it in public. How would that make you feel?

God wants to do great things in your life. God wants to work miracles. God wants to give you graces beyond belief. It would be a great insult to Him to keep His work hidden as if it's a dark secret.

The culture in America today is very much anti-Christian. And as long as good Christians are afraid to open their mouths, the culture will continue to intimidate the righteous. The only way to fight it is to proudly proclaim your alliance with Christ.

Now let's look at the list:

1. You are praying every day.
2. You are confessing your sins to a priest in a reasonable amount of time.
3. You are giving an accountability partner scheduled updates.
4. You are being honest and apologetic with your spouse, without burdening her with details.
5. You have specific responses to specific temptations, you know what they are, and you practice them constantly.
6. You don't think about your response—you just do it.

7. You keep destructive media out of your home and (as much as possible) out of your place of work.
8. You make every act of sex committed to God and your wife, allowing the possibility for children if it is God's will.
9. You cherish your wife and every night ask yourself if you've cherished her as Jesus cherishes His church.
10. You know your triggers and have prepared responses to them.
11. You keep a list of friends to call... and use them as often as necessary.
12. You are always looking for ways to please God more.
13. You glorify God by 'spreading the Word.'

Chapter 11 – Avoid Traps

If you're truly trying to accept God in your life, if you're fighting all of Satan's lies, if you're doing all you can to stay pure, then you can count on two things: #1 – God will help you. #2 – The Devil will do everything he can to bring you down. Accepting God means painting a huge target on your chest. In a war, sharp shooters will always shoot for the officers and leaders of an army. In the spiritual battle you've entered, the enemy will do everything to keep you from leading more souls to heaven.

Remember that Satan has been developing traps for man since man's creation. He used one when he first convinced Adam and Eve to discover sin in the Garden of Eden. He used one when he convinced men to crucify Christ instead of worship Him. He used one when he first introduced you to pornography. And he will use many more to get you to look at pornography again.

In the first part of this book, I told you about the different stages of purity... and the traps that you'll encounter as you move through these stages. Now I'll tell you how to avoid and overcome them.

Avoiding Despair

Despair is probably the hardest of all traps to avoid. Despair is the overwhelming sadness you might feel, even as you are succeeding in your struggle, which fools you into thinking there is no hope. That despite your success, the devil will get to you in the end. That there's really no point in trying. It is the time in which you will ask yourself, "Why bother? Life still sucks even without the porn."

You might feel some of this during your withdraw period, but you'll probably feel it most strongly during your testing period—the point at which you are over the honeymoon stage. You must now resume your daily living routines *without* those 'cloud nine' feelings... but also without slipping back into your old habit of self-medication.

Sadly, there's not much you can do about the depressing feelings you go through—not as prescribed in this book anyway. If your depression or anxiety is too severe, you might have to talk to a doctor about it.

But depression is different than despair. Depression is the sadness you feel. Despair is giving in to that sadness. Giving in to the temptation to quit because you feel there's no hope.

The last thing anyone going through hardship wants to hear is lectures about Job and other men of the Bible who went through trials. About the good God will bring out of your struggles. Yes, it's all true, but when we're in our slumps, it's irritating to listen to someone else tell us about it. So I won't do that. Instead, I'll try to give you some things to try during those hard times—hoping you'll get through it and meet me on the other side.

Foundations

Before going into the defenses against despair, it's important that you understand how much of a foundation Christ should be throughout all of this. Think of the house you live in. The floors, the walls, the ceiling. The carpet, the paint, the lights. The furniture, the decorations, computer and television. They all serve different functions in your home. They all do something, whether it's functional as part of the home or more of a luxury to enhance the home. But none of them would be there (the home itself would not stand) without a strong foundation.

You have many things in your life that will help you through struggles. But all of it must be supported by Christ, the Church, and the sacraments. That is why the first two steps described in this book are the most important. Without God, nothing can exist. Without God, you will never really recover from your addiction. Even if you never looked at pornography again, you cannot really recover unless God is supporting you.

There are so many times you will not feel God in your life (and more to the point, you will not feel Him in your struggle against porn). You won't *notice* His presence. Just as you walk throughout your home and not think of or notice the foundation that is supporting it all. But if He's there (if you've based all that you do on His mercy and love) then you can *know* He is present.

This means that you will accept nothing that does not please God. As you struggle with despair, you will be tempted to do things that might *seem* to help the situation. But for everything you do, you should always refer back to the test: *is this action directly pleasing to God*? If not, then you know that it will not help you in your struggle against pornography. For example, you might (in a moment of despair) decide to have a few beers to kind of smooth out your emotional turmoil. Not that a few beers are wrong, but if you're using chemicals to create a mood that doesn't exist (the mood of fun or tranquility), then you know you're not using them properly. You're abusing one thing in order to avoid abusing something else. Alcohol for sex. It won't work. I'll go more into that in the upcoming section on "substituting." The point here is that abusing alcohol (or any other chemical) is not pleasing to God. Therefore, you can know with certainty that it will not help you in your recovery.

Always return to your foundation when considering how to react to depression. If it doesn't fit within the foundational reason for your recovery, then don't do it.

Fellowship

Now as for some tips to help you deal directly with the temptation to despair, your first line of defense (once again) is going to be your accountability partners and other men in the group you've joined. Remember that chapter? Remember when I kept telling you how important fellowship was? This is why.

I myself am very prone to despair. As a matter of fact, I'm one of the worse quitters. Every time something goes wrong in a project, I think of it as a reason to give up and walk away. That's probably why I have so many hobbies. I stay with one long enough to learn a few things, and then walk away from it the second I might really start to get somewhere.

I'm reminded of a car I once bought. It had a blown engine, but the purchase came with a new engine block. All I had to do was swap them. Yeah. That's *all* I had to do.

I was employed at a garage (I wasn't a mechanic—I mainly did oil changes and brake jobs), so I would work on the project after my shift. I spent hours and hours tearing that car apart, and ten times as many hours putting it back together.

There were times I got so frustrated that I'd grab anything I could find and throw it at the car. A wrench, a screw driver, even a rock. The paint had quite a few scratches in it when I finished.

And every time I'd get upset and throw something, I'd back away from it and say, "That's it! I'm done with this piece of garbage." Well, maybe my words were a little bit more colorful. It *was* a garage.

Fortunately, I had formed some good friendships with the other men who worked there—the real technicians. They'd see me get angry. They'd keep their distance for a few minutes. And finally, they'd walk over and point out a couple of things. Maybe something I was doing wrong, or just something that might make it easier. Sometimes, they'd just encourage me to get back on the horse. To keep going, even if I'm fed up with the car. Even if I felt like it wasn't worth my time and effort. Just a simple, "Take a smoke break and get back to work," was enough to motivate me back into action.

That's not to say you want to dump on your accountability partners every five minutes about every problem in your life. But in those really desperate hours, sometimes you need to just call someone and say, "Hey, I don't like this. I really feel like giving up."

And then your accountability partner can say, "Hey, none of us like it—but you have to fight anyway. That's part of being a man. You're a man. You've made it this far. You'll have to roll up your sleeves and get back to work."

That alone can get you back into the game sometimes. No, it won't make your problems disappear. It probably won't even make you feel better about your problems. But it will let you

160

know that life is livable. That you *can* get through this. Even if it's hard, you have the ability to be the man God wants you to be... that He *expects* you to be. That your struggles aren't all for nothing, but that they will harden your resolve and soften your heart.

Prayer and Scripture

During those harsh months, it's also good to have some inspiring Bible verses to read and contemplate. Scripture is there for us to study, to learn about God, to learn the right way of living, and to learn about each other. But it also can (and should) inspire us.

Prayer is essential to getting through depression and anxiety. Without it, sadness becomes despair very quickly. But you should pay attention to the way you pray to God. It's easy to dump on God, the way we would a friend. And while there's nothing specifically wrong with telling God about your problems, you don't want to internally trap yourself into a "poor me" attitude. You want to make sure you are praying to God, and not just brooding or pouting.

One of the templates or models I like to use is ACTS (Adoration, Confession, Thanksgiving, and Supplication).

Adoration: We often forget to spend time adoring Christ. He is above all. He is the Truth and the Light and the Way. We must give that attention. Adoration helps us focus on God's greatness instead of our own weakness. Sometimes, though, this isn't easy. There have been so many times I was tempted to say to God, "Well, if you're so great, why can't you help me with this?" But I resisted those temptations and instead said, "God, I cannot comprehend your greatness because my mind is small. But I accept it. Help me to know you in time, so that I may never think my will is better than yours."

Confession: Confession to God is something you should be doing daily. But throughout the day, as you utter prayers, it's good to admit to the faults within the past several hours. The improper stares. The harsh words to your family, coworkers, or friends. Whatever—just remember that you can't fool God. He knows what you've done already. But He can only forgive you when you've admitted it and confessed it to Him.

Thanksgiving: How often do you offer thanks to God? If you're anything like me, you forget to do it in most of your prayers. I myself have so much to be grateful for. I think if I spent more time thanking God for the good things I had, and less time wining about the things I don't have, I'd realize how foolish I am.

Supplication: Supplication is the petition—always mindful that His will is more important than our desires.

Other Activities

I had mentioned earlier (several times) that you should have some sort of hobby to fall back on. An activity that you can use to kind of break the depression and anxiety. This hobby will greatly reduce the temptation to despair.

But you also must be careful not to use your hobby as a means of escape. Spending hours and hours on something that pulls you away from reality is not good for your recovery. Take your hobby in small time units. Enough to get you somewhat excited about the project you're doing. As you feel some of the depression letting up, then break away from it so that you can once again join your normal life—only with a refreshed sense of accomplishment (or hope for accomplishment) instead of a hopeless sense of dread.

Helping Others

Even the secular world recognizes that helping others and giving your time away in charity is an awesome way to break away from self-pity. The problem is, you can't always just ditch what you're doing to go serve food in a soup kitchen or read to old people at a nursing home. But there are very few times when you can't find *anyone* to be charitable to. At work, at home, wherever—the opportunity for charity is a full barrel when you know where to look.

When I worked for a garage, cleaning the shop was one of my duties. Every now and then, just to break the monotony, I would clean up around one of the technician's toolboxes. And if I had time, I might even clean and wax the toolbox itself. Cleaning a coworker's toolbox was a huge step outside of my normal duties. But you can bet not one person complained when I did it.

When I worked in a shop as one of three copier technicians, I would sometimes pick up a parts order for one of the other technicians and fill it for him (that was one of those mundane jobs that we all had to do but no one enjoyed). No one ever complained about that one either.

When I worked on the road as a copier tech, it was harder to find coworkers to help out. Charity isn't quite as easy when you're on your own all day. But then again, if you know where to look, charity can get awful easy. I worked in the downtown area, so I always made sure to carry a few extra bucks to give to pan-handlers. If I didn't have money, I would give them a few cigarettes out of my pack... even if that meant I'd be short at the end of the day. Giving away something that I would miss made me feel that much better about myself and my situation. And no one complained about it.

At home, charity takes on a slightly different dimension. Often, it feels more like a duty than an act of charity. For example, doing the dishes, when normally your wife or one of the kids does them. It just feels like a chore. Especially when no one notices or comments on it. And helping your children with something or even doing special things for your children will very rarely feel like charity, since most kids are just open mouths ready to have charity spooned (or shoveled) into them... always taking and taking and taking.

But you can do a few things to make such tasks feel *more* like charitable acts. You can do them with a smile, even when you hate doing them. You can pay compliments (to your spouse or your kids) before and after doing them. Pay a special compliment to your wife about the dinner she made—tell her it was so good you're going to do the dishes for her. She won't complain.

These little things aren't always going to put you on cloud nine and make you feel like the world is just a lovely place to be. But they can make it all just a little more livable. And remember—your depression isn't going to last forever. There will be a day when you wake up and think, "Wow, this really isn't so bad. I think I've got it pretty good." Until then, you'll have to do with, "I can get through this... God is on my side."

Avoiding Rationalization

Rationalization: to bring into accord with reason or cause something to seem reasonable: as to attribute (one's actions) to rational and creditable motives without analysis of true and especially unconscious motives.[24]

If you're looking at women (whether it's nude women online or half-dressed women at the beach), it's because you lust after them and aren't controlling your passions. If you claim to have other reasons, you're rationalizing. Plain and simple. And you should avoid rationalization at all costs.

Sitting at my computer, in the middle of the night, while my wife is at work, this is what was going through my mind:

"This isn't all that bad. I mean, I'm not hurting anyone. And anyway, if my wife would give me a little more, or pay a little more attention to me, I wouldn't be looking for it elsewhere. It's practically her fault. And besides, God gave me these desires. He made me want them so much that I would have to have them—that I wouldn't feel right until I'd gone all the way. If He didn't want me to do this, then He shouldn't have given me such a strong desire. Still—I can stop right now. If God wants me to stop right now, He'll make the next page I click on be about religion or something. He can do anything, so He can at least do that. If it's

---

[24] http://www.merriam-webster.com/dictionary/rationalization

164

about religion, I'll stop what I'm doing and get down and pray. It's up to God now and not me—see? So God must not care because this page isn't about religion, or anything related to religion."

If you go through a jailhouse, you can meet hundreds of hardened criminals—men who have committed some of the most awful crimes. But very few of them will say that there's no such thing as right and wrong. Very few of them would say that *anyone* should be allowed to do *anything*. What most of them will say is that *they* were justified in *their* crimes because of specific circumstances. The crime was wrong, except for them. When we choose to rationalize, when we ignore what we know is right and exchange that for a warped logic that justifies what we want, we can do some of the craziest things without feeling culpable.

During the years you grew into a pornography habit, you probably did quite a bit of rationalizing. And if you start rationalizing again, even for the small things, you'll be right back where you were.

One of the biggest rationalizations for recovering porn addicts is, "It's unreasonable to say that I can't look at *any* women. I mean, that's half the population. How can I avoid looking at half the population? Checking out the receptionist at this office is a far cry from looking at pornography and masturbating. She *wants* to be checked out; otherwise she wouldn't have dressed this way. And God wants me to appreciate His creation. This isn't wrong. This isn't impure. This is just life."

This kind of thinking will always leave the door open for the next step. Once you tell yourself that something isn't sinful (when you know in your heart that it is), you make the next part seem *less* sinful. Think of the process as a number of levels:

1. You see a girl. (no sin has been committed yet)
2. You turn to glance at her again. (the first venial sin has now been committed)

3. You stare at her. (the venial sin is now coaxing you to something more)
4. You turn away but continue to think about her, not trying to stop. (you're bordering on mortal sin now)
5. You begin to imagine her without clothes. (now you've crossed the line)
6. You go home and try to find her on Facebook—or search for images of women with the same look or build. (it's pretty obvious where this is going)

Once you've justified level 2, then level 3 seems like not such a big deal. After all, how different is a glance from a stare? And if you rationalized that behavior, then level 4 is really easy to justify as well.

The key to this is to cut yourself off at level 1. You saw a girl, now leave it at that. If you've followed the directions in the chapter on changing your reaction to the sight of women (if you've formed the habit of looking away) then you will actually have to *think* about looking back again. You will have to rationalize to get to level 2. You'll need a reason to look at her.

Cut off your brain at this time. Don't argue with yourself. Remember—she's forbidden. You have no *right* to look at her. You're not going to be reasonable about. You're just going to look away. There's nothing to talk about. There's nothing to think about. So don't.

Avoiding Substitutes

Did you know that Sears used to sell heroin as an alternative for morphine. It was also supposed to be a cure for alcoholism. We all know how that ended. The newest cure for heroin is methadone. Junkies have to stand in long lines to receive the legal medication—the medication which has almost the same effects as heroin does.

I'm not a doctor, and I don't pretend to know everything there is about drug addiction; but it seems like such substitution just leads people in a vicious circle. It never addresses the real problem. It never actually cleans anyone up.

Substitution might be necessary (at least for a time) when it comes to drug addiction because of the severe withdraw symptoms. But we're not dealing with heart failures, vomiting, and convulsions when we deal with pornography withdrawal. So substitution is out of the question. You need strength—not crutches.

Keep a careful inventory of your daily activities. Watch for signs that you are substituting. If you're spending too much time on any sort of recreation or entertainment, you should back off. You don't want to get so involved into something that it becomes another means for escape. Especially something that isn't productive or constructive.

Of course, you might find yourself more heavily involved in a hobby. This is usually healthy, as long as you're not letting your hobby stand between your duties as a father or husband. Remember that you must spend time with your family. Isolating yourself doesn't help you overcome temptation—it makes temptation worse.

If you think you might be substituting (even for something constructive) then start timing yourself. If necessary, set up a schedule. Fill your schedule with all the necessary duties first. Work, family time, prayer (don't ever forget to schedule prayer time), sleep, etc.,. Then you can see how much time is left for recreation.

Video games and television are two of the most popular substitutes... especially for younger men. Did you know that the brain behaves the same way when a person is being hypnotized as when they are watching TV or playing video games? There have been hundreds of studies proving it. If you substitute either of these for sexual addiction, then how can you expect to hold up against temptation? Screen time absolutely drains your power of discernment. What's more, you'll have a hard time finding any totally clean television content—even if you're watching kid shows. Clean is what you need right now, and television has none of that.

Drinking is also a common substitute, since men feel less sexually driven while under the influence. But drinking, like television, interferes with our will. It makes rationalization so much easier. In fact, it's a quick ride to sin. Don't do it. I would suggest abstaining from alcohol completely until you've got some clean time under your belt.

Avoiding Complacency

Complacency is the big trap for men who are far along in their recovery. It is the trap that will lie in wait for you for the rest of your life. It is the one that hits while you aren't looking—aren't expecting. Avoiding complacency is the most important part of your maintenance stage.

Once you've gotten through the first stages of recovery, you rejoin life. You experience the everyday ups and downs. You find a sense of normality again. It is then that you are tempted to think you have the problem licked.

"I've been clean for almost a year," you might say. "In fact, I sometimes wonder why I ever had any problem at all. I pass girls in all kinds of inappropriate clothing, and I hardly ever even look. I spend time on the internet and I never stray from the righteous path. And if something does 'pop up,' I look away immediately. I feel kind of silly for having ever thought of pornography as a problem."

The reason it's so easy to feel this way is because the pain and trouble you've caused (caused for yourself and caused for others) is no longer fresh in your mind. You don't remember the long hours you wasted. You don't remember the guilt you carried around with you. You don't remember your wife's tears when you told her about it. You might not even remember the deep sense of humiliation and shame you felt when you first began talking about it with other men. The self-loathing. The denial. The extreme turmoil your emotional, mental, physical, and spiritual self was put through. It's all forgotten.

Retrain Yourself

If you've followed the directions in this book, you've picked up certain habits. When you see a woman, especially an attractive one who is inappropriately dressed, your eyes immediately dart away. You should have programmed this behavior into yourself by now. So you actually have to think about taking that second look. This was difficult to do, and it took time (probably with a lot of failures). But now that you've reached this point, you've stopped thinking about how much women tempted you when you *didn't* have the habit.

Here's something you should always remember: it took a couple of months to form the habit, but it would only take a few days to lose it. That's right, we slip into a habit of sin much more quickly than we train ourselves to develop virtue. If you've lost the habit of looking away, go back and reread the chapter on "Change The Habit". Retrain yourself, and stick with those practices constantly. Without the habit of controlling your eyes and your thoughts, the complacency will quickly push you all the way back to square one.

Create A Memorial

It was a cold day, and snow was falling on the ground. I had spent all the last night (in freezing weather) working on my wife's car, installing a new alternator. She was on her way to work now, and I had to take the kids to school before going to work myself.

But the kids weren't cooperating. There were fights, there was playing, and there was stalling. I needed them to get in the van and hit the road, and these kids didn't seem to get it. If I had one nerve left in my body, they were on it. By the time I had gotten them to my vehicle, I was yelling. By the time I had them in their seats and had shut the door, I was cussing under my breath.

And still, they would not just sit down and shut up!

Then my wife calls me on the cell phone. Her car broke down again, and she was in the middle of the road. Now I had to get the kids to school, get her to work, find a way to get the broken car off the road, and get to work myself... all within the next hour. And I had ten bucks in my bank account—that's it.

My blood was boiling at that point and I started screaming at the kids, telling them to (for heaven's sake) just sit the @#$% down and shut the @#$% up! When they didn't, I threw a tantrum. I picked up a book and threw it at one child. I spanked one and smacked another.

Then I uttered the unforgiveable words, "I hate you! I hate you all!"

This incident, it would seem, had nothing to do with pornography. But then again, it all went back to pornography.

Life constantly throws curveballs at us. Hardships that can sometimes be very difficult to bear. As men of God, we see them as tests. We put our heads down and face the wind as well as we can. But as men of sin, we lack the strength to get through such hardships. As men of sin, we cry and scream and lay down on the floor and kick like babies. I had become such a slave to my passion that I was living in absolute despair. I hated myself, I hated my life. My anger, partly caused by my deep feelings of guilt and shame, was constantly bubbling out of control. And now I had crossed a line I never thought I would cross. And I had done irreparable damage. My children, to this day, have never forgotten those words.

Most of the recovered men I know can think of some point in their lives where their sin had climaxed—where they had reached a point in which they realized just how out-of-hand things had gotten. This was *my* climax. This is the point in my life when I knew that I absolutely *must* find a way out of my self-created prison.

Every time I'm tempted to sin, I try to remember this incident. I say to myself, "Do you want to go back there? If you sin, this is where it will lead. Maybe not immediately, but you will eventually reach this state again and you might not ever recover. The kids might not ever recover. In fact, it will probably get even

170

worse than this. Don't step in that direction—not even an inch. Stay in the light."

You will eventually be so far into your recovery, that you've forgotten the deep pain you felt when you were stumbling around in that darkness. While you certainly want to move on with your life (enjoying the virtues you've learned, thanking God for them, and getting over all the sins you've committed), you must never forget where you came from.

Most cultures (including our American culture) have certain rituals they go through to commemorate good or bad times in history. They also erect structures to serve as reminders. We have war memorials all over the place. Some of them dedicated to entire wars, some to battles, and some even to specific soldiers. We also have memorials to remember things like slavery—the atrocities committed against fellow men and the great sacrifice it took to end slavery in America.

Such memorials (whether it's a structure, a service, or even a holiday) are important in life. They keep us from forgetting that the easy life we have (easy, that is, compared to what it could be) wasn't free. They also give us a certain amount of respect for (or even fear of) the circumstances that formed our culture.

You're walking in the light. You've been in the light so long that you don't even clearly remember the darkness and how it affected you. You need a memorial, if nothing else, so that you can occasionally look back at that darkness and remember what it did to you.

Journals are great memorials. That's why it's good to start journaling early. So that once you're far into the journey, you can turn back the pages and see what a great struggle it was. See how much you've accomplished. See how terrible it would be to return to that ugly spot once again.

If there's an incident that "woke you up," then write about it. Put it on paper, so that you can always look back on it and see just how important it is for you to stay in the light.

Help Others

I told you from the start, you're not in this battle alone. Every man struggles with lust. Every man is tempted by the female body. Some (many in fact) have fallen into the same darkness you were in. They need help, just as you did.

You can find other men online in pornography addiction forums. You can find them in support groups. You might even have a few friends who need help. You can't force help on someone—trying to do that will only frustrate you... and often will lead you back to acting out. But for those who want help, who have decided to live in the light, *they* will actually help *you* overcome complacency. When they share their struggles and the self loathing you once felt, it will remind you of what it was like when you were there. When they share their joy of overcoming their temptations, you yourself will experience a small part of it... remembering your *own* victories in battle.

As it will with depression, being there for others will help you overcome complacency. As a matter of fact, it's almost necessary to overcome complacency. It's part of your maintenance stage, and it goes right back to what I had said before: you cannot hide the light of Christ. If you try to cover the light that Christ gives you, you will smother the flame and it will go out entirely.

Stay With Your Group

Whether it's to find others to help or to serve as your own personal memorial, you *must* stay with a support group. Consider this part of your life—not just a phase.

No one is perfect. You will have failures. Even if you never look at pornography again, you will be wounded by sin. It might be a girl that you stared at. It might be a picture you looked at. It might be old images in your mind that popped up out of nowhere, and you allowed yourself to think about them for a while before pushing them out of your head. It might be just putting yourself in the occasion of sin, pursuing situations where you might 'accidentally' see something. Or it might be something unrelated to pornography. But these failures (no matter how small) will eventually lead you back to the same sinful lifestyle if you do not have support and accountability.

You can report these failures in the beginning, while they're still small and controllable, or you can hide them— allowing them to fester and grow. But if you hide them, you'll eventually have to go back to that support group with a depressing report. You'll kind of feel like a dog, when it's guilty of something and has its tail between its legs. You don't want to feel that way... not after having made so much progress. Reporting your failures early will help you avoid that—as well as stifling the complacency you feel.

Remember, the men in your group have been there. They know what failure is. They know what success is. They're there for support in both cases. If you stop going, they can't help you, whether you're trying to recover from sin or maintain your purity.

Now where are we in our list:

1. You are praying every day.
2. You are confessing your sins to a priest in a reasonable amount of time.
3. You are giving an accountability partner scheduled updates.
4. You are being honest and apologetic with your spouse, without burdening her with details.
5. You have specific responses to specific temptations, you know what they are, and you practice them constantly.
6. You don't think about your response—you just do it.
7. You keep destructive media out of your home and (as much as possible) out of your place of work.
8. You make every act of sex committed to God and your wife, allowing the possibility for children if it is God's will.

9. You cherish your wife and every night ask yourself if you've cherished her as Jesus cherishes His church.
10. You know your triggers and have prepared responses to them.
11. You keep a list of friends to call... and use them as often as necessary.
12. You are always looking for ways to please God more.
13. You glorify God by 'spreading the Word.'
14. You are vigilant against despair, rationalization, substituting, and complacency. You have a planned strategy against every one of these traps.

Chapter 12 – Bounce Back From Failure

Wouldn't it be nice to never be tempted again? To not have to worry about our lust, our anger, our gluttony, or our laziness? To know that we'll always be pleasing to God, and nothing can take it away. To know we'll always make the right decisions, even when those decisions are difficult?

Well, let's get back to the real world. That's not going to happen. None of it. God will help us. God will strengthen us. But usually, our strength comes from dealing with (and overcoming) temptation. And since we can't make the temptations disappear (along with the fact that we aren't perfect) we're also going to have to deal with failure. In this war, we will be wounded. It might be a little slip up, it might be a big one. But we will all have them.

The question is, how do we bounce back?

Reacting To Failure

Let's start with your immediate reaction to failure. You may have already developed some patterns in your reaction, and maybe they are destructive. My own reaction to failure (whether it was a big failure or a small one) was to medicate... with drugs. In fact, I had grown into this pattern so much, that often I didn't even fight the temptation to look at pornography because I knew, in the back of my mind, that I had a large supply of drugs and would be able to escape my guilt and shame for a long time. Obviously, this behavior created a vicious cycle. The only way to break it (since I can't be 100% fail-free) was to find a new way to deal with myself once I had fallen.

Guilt is a way for our God-given conscience to say, "You did something wrong. Shame on you." We shouldn't run from guilt. We shouldn't mask it. In fact, we should try to nourish it. But at the same time, we don't want to be handcuffed to the guilt.

Look at the first two steps to breaking porn in this book. Chapters 5 and 6. They can be used to deal with specific sins as well as the pornography addiction itself. Using them will help you channel your guilt into something that can help you (God actually meant for guilt to help you) rather than something that will bring you down further into sin. Start by following these steps:

Recognize the sin, admit to the sin, and shine light on the sin.

You must come to terms with the fact that you are wounded. If you don't (if you completely ignore the guilty feeling) you leave a gaping wound in your flesh, and it will kill you spiritually. So admit that you have done something sinful as early as possible.

Then call your accountability partner. Tell him the nature of your sin, without giving so much detail that it will tempt him into sin. You don't want to drone on about it for too long. Just letting him know that you have had a slipup and are trying to recover from that is enough for now. The next chance you get, go to confession and receive absolution.

There—you've recognized your sin, admitted that it was your own failure, and confessed it. And depending on the gravity of the sin, you might need to tell your wife about it. Remember, your wounds are hers. She is affected by your actions, and she has a right to know.

From there, you should try to distract yourself for a while. Not to escape the guilt, but to keep it from making you despair. A hobby, your work, or some chores. Remember that an idle mind is the devil's workshop. If you sit around and think about your failure, you will probably only be tempted to fail again. And again and again.

Learning From Failure

When some of the guilt has passed, and you can think clearly again, then consider all that led up to your failure. If you've been clean for a while, then this slipup probably didn't come out of nowhere. There were circumstances that either created an opportunity or heightened your temptations.

Did you do something beforehand that would give you a special opportunity to pursue pornography? Were you on the prowl for temptations? Most men (especially those who are making special efforts to purify their lives) find themselves actively seeking circumstances where they might 'accidentally' see something they shouldn't. Watching a movie they know will have sex scenes. Looking through something or searching for something on the internet. Peeping through a spouse's magazines. All in the hopes that they'll catch a glimpse of skin.

But often, the real failure started even before they were actually pursuing temptation. Often, they will have fallen short in their control of the eyes. Perhaps they give in on one day, and look over a girl they see at work. The next day they give in twice. And so on, until they've completely lost control of their eyes. Is this you? Where did you think it would lead?

The temptation might also have been a trigger and not so much part of your sex drive. Were you following the steps to fight triggers and control your reaction to them? Did you allow yourself to sit idly, thinking about your problems and soaking in despair? Did you talk yourself into a feeling of entitlement after a fight with your wife?

Take a hard look at yourself and don't play mind games. You fell for a reason. What was that reason? And how are you going to fix it so you don't fall again?

Bouncing Back

You've admitted to your sin, you've confessed it, and you've taken a look at your actions leading up to your sin. Now it's time to outline a game-plan so that it doesn't happen again. It's time to *bounce*, instead of hitting the ground and staying there.

If this is the second time you've hit the ground (or the third or the fourth or the thousandth), don't get discouraged. You spent a long time developing your porn addiction. It's probably not going to disappear all in one day. Chin-up, man-up, and let's focus on the solution.

Wherever you went wrong, find the corresponding chapter (or chapters) in this book and reread it. A lot of times, we can get so used to a virtue (it becomes so much a part of our life) that we forget how we ever obtained that virtue. For example, you might have done really well with eye control. You developed the habit of looking away immediately whenever you sensed a temptation. After a while, you didn't even think about it anymore. Your body just reacted the way you had trained it to. And then, through complacency, you allowed yourself to take those second glances. Over and over you did this, until, over time, you lost the habit of looking away. Now you have to go back and rediscover how you first obtained that habit. The tips and tricks you used to develop it.

Changing The Battle Plan

Sometimes, you need to refocus your techniques. Let's say you never really got the hang of looking away from women. You only learned semi-control, but it was enough, for a while, to fight off the really strong urges. But now it's not working. Now you're acting out, and you've identified this area as your weakness.

Start at the beginning again and reread the chapters that would help you. Usually, one or two of the techniques will really 'click' with someone. Which ones clicked for you? Those might have worked for a while, but maybe you should try harder with the techniques that *didn't* click with you.

You might need some outside advice if you don't know where you're going wrong. This is another reason you should stay with a support group long after you've entered into the maintenance stage of your recovery.

I remember once sharing at my support group that I was having particular trouble at church. It was very difficult for me to get through a Mass without 'checking out' the girls in front of me.

Especially the ones wearing tight pants, tight dresses, or high shorts.

One of the members of my group simply said, "Try sitting in the front pew."'

There—problem solved. It also gave my children a better chance to observe and participate in the Mass.

My point is that sometimes there are very simple solutions to difficult problems. Many of those solutions are in this book. But you'll find many more when you share your experiences with other men and listen to them share theirs.

You also might have to reconsider points that you rejected in the beginning of this battle. For example, I heard one man share that he didn't think a "TOTAL PURE" approach was practical. He needed to break himself from pornography (the kind in print and on the internet) before he could worry about the smaller things, like checking out girls. Not that he wouldn't *try* to stop checking out girls, but his focus would have to be on the big things, not the little things.

I didn't interrupt him, or correct him. That's not for me to do. But I knew that at some point in his struggle, he'd have to realize that the little things are *feeding* the big things. He thought a total purity approach was impossible because it seemed like such a huge change in his life. He didn't yet realize that once you deal with the little things (checking out girls as they walk by), then the big thing (pornography and masturbation) is starved to the point that you can easily overcome it. Work small, change big.

There are probably other points in this book (or points you've heard from other people) that your mind immediately rejected. They seemed unreasonable when you read them and they didn't fit within your scope. They required something from other people and you didn't think those other people would cooperate. They asked you to make drastic changes in your life that didn't seem fair.

But if you're not succeeding in your struggle against pornography, then maybe it's time to have a fresh look at those things and reconsider them.

In the first stages of my recovery, I didn't understand how support groups would help. To me, it seemed silly. Getting up in front of people and uttering those all-to-cliché words, "Hi—I'm Eric and I'm a porn addict." How is that going to help me?

But at the same time, I had come to accept the fact that I could not be trusted to follow my own way of thinking. I had been trying to kick the habit for years on my own and couldn't get anywhere. For once in my life, it was time for me to completely rely on the advice of an outside source. So I forced myself to attend the meetings each week. They were uncomfortable at first. I felt weird (like a freak of nature) being there. But I continued, because I knew I couldn't rely on myself.

I'm so thankful that I swallowed my pride on that point. Without my support group, I would not have made it. Not even for a few weeks.

So if you're still struggling, try to think of all you've been told by others and have rejected in your mind. You may have missed a very important element of the recovery process. You might be thinking inside the box, and that box obviously isn't big enough.

Now for our list:

1. You are praying every day.
2. You are confessing your sins to a priest in a reasonable amount of time.
3. You are giving an accountability partner scheduled updates.
4. You are being honest and apologetic with your spouse, without burdening her with details.
5. You have specific responses to specific temptations, you know what they are, and you practice them constantly.
6. You don't think about your response—you just do it.
7. You keep destructive media out of your home and (as much as possible) out of your place of work.

8. You make every act of sex committed to God and your wife, allowing the possibility for children if it is God's will.
9. You cherish your wife and every night ask yourself if you've cherished her as Jesus cherishes His church.
10. You know your triggers and have prepared responses to them.
11. You keep a list of friends to call... and use them as often as necessary.
12. You are always looking for ways to please God more.
13. You glorify God by 'spreading the Word.'
14. You are vigilant against despair, rationalization, substituting, and complacency. You have a planned strategy against every one of these traps.
15. You take failures in stride and do not overlook them, but do not let them cause despair either.

Chapter 13 – Thank God

And as he entered into a certain town, there met him ten men that were lepers, who stood afar off.

And lifted up their voice, saying: Jesus, Master, have mercy on us.

Whom when he saw, he said: Go, shew yourselves to the priests. And it came to pass, as they went, they were made clean.

And one of them, when he saw that he was made clean, went back, with a loud voice glorifying God.

And he fell on his face before his feet, giving thanks. And this was a Samaritan.

And Jesus answering, said: Were not ten made clean? And where are the nine?

There is no one found to return and give glory to God, but this stranger.

And he said to him: Arise, go thy way; for thy faith hath made thee whole.[25]

What do you think those other nine lepers were thinking to themselves, as they walked away from Jesus? Obviously, they recognized Jesus as having some authority and of having great power. They didn't ask to be healed—they asked for mercy. But when they were healed, they all knew where that healing had come from. So why didn't they all return to give thanks?

---

[25] Luke 17:12-19

I used to sit and wonder about that. Here are a few things they might have been thinking:

"He didn't tell us to come back and thank Him. He told us to go to the priests, so we have to do that first."

"Maybe we'll come back and thank Him later—after we're sure we're cured. We really don't know if we're actually better yet. Not until we've been examined by the priests."

"We'll thank Him in our hearts."

"He knows we're grateful. We don't have to say it."

I can only guess at their thoughts because I've used these lies many times myself. Yes—they're all excuses not to do what's right. The one leper was overcome with joy at being healed. He didn't need proof. He didn't need the approval of someone else. He knew that he felt better and he knew that Jesus was the cause of it. And he acted on that.

Such must your reaction be to purity. You didn't achieve it on your own. You had help. Possibly help from other people, but definitely help from God. You must acknowledge this, and you must act on it. Not just in your heart with a small prayer of gratitude, but with an overflowing joy that gives glory to God. And don't ever stop. If you've been clean for one day or one year or one hundred years, you owe that to God. And if God put people in your life to help you in your struggle, thank Him for those people. If this book has helped you, then thank God for this book (I only wrote it because I felt God had asked me to... so all of it really goes back to Him). Everything good that you have, you owe to Him. Thank Him for it all.

Thanking God Privately

Fasting and prayer are two powerful weapons against the enemy. We use them (or should use them) constantly to help us avoid sin and do God's will. In fact, sometimes is it our only defense. The apostles discovered this when they were trying to cast a stubborn demon out of a man.

And one of the multitude, answering, said: Master, I have brought my son to thee, having a dumb spirit.

Who, wheresoever he taketh him, dasheth him: and he foameth and gnasheth with the teeth and pineth away.

And I spoke to thy disciples to cast him out: and they could not.

Who answering them, said: O incredulous generation, how long shall I be with you? How long shall I suffer you? Bring him unto me.

And they brought him. And when he had seen him, immediately the spirit troubled him and being thrown down upon the ground, he rolled about foaming.

And he asked his father: How long time is it since this hath happened unto him? But he sad: From his infancy.

And oftentimes hath he cast him into the fire and into the waters to destroy him. But if thou canst do any thing, help us, having compassion on us.

And Jesus saith to him: If thou canst believe, all things are possible to him that believeth.

And immediately the father of the boy crying out, with tears said: I do believe, Lord. Help my unbelief.

And when Jesus saw the multitude running together, he threatened the unclean spirit, saying to him: Deaf and dumb spirit, I command thee, go out of him and enter not any more into him.

And crying out and greatly tearing him, he went out of him. And he became as dead, so that many said: He is dead.

But Jesus taking him by the hand, lifted him up. And he arose.

And when he was come into the house, his disciples secretly asked him: Why could not we cast him out?

*And he said to them: **This kind can go out by nothing, but by prayer and fasting.**[26]*

When we fast, we usually do it for a specific cause. We need help spiritually. We want God to help someone else. He have financial troubles. We have injuries or sickness. Or we want to help someone else with sickness.

Now think about this: if prayer and fasting holds the answer to difficult circumstances, wouldn't that also be a great answer to thanksgiving? You might have fasted for many things in the past, but how often have you fasted and offered up your suffering in thanksgiving?

Such a private devotion would be well received by our Savior. It would truly glorify God, more than any "thank you" ever could. It goes completely against the way we've learned to think. On Thanksgiving Day, we celebrate our prosperity with enormous feasts. What if we celebrated with a meager drink of water and a few crumbs of bread?

---

[26] Mark 9:17-29

Set a specific day of the month (or day of the week, if you're that ambitious about giving thanks) to fast, offering up everything that day in thanksgiving.

Thanking God Publicly

When God does something for us, He wants us to thank Him privately in our own hearts. But remember what we talked about before—about letting the light of God shine forth. God wants public recognition as well. But in this specific situation, you don't necessarily want everyone to know exactly *what* God did for you. As mentioned in previous chapters, this is a delicate subject matter. Even if you no longer feel shame about it, you should feel some shame in sharing it with certain people... especially women. Your sexual sins should be guarded. We're not supposed to display them, even if we're beyond them now and no longer take part in them.

So how do you give public thanks to God, without putting your past sins on display for everyone to see?

Let's start with the fact that God has done more for you than free you from pornography. He gave you family and friends. He gave you gifts and talents. He gave you a way to earn a living for yourself and anyone you support. He gave you sight and hearing. He gave you legs to walk on and arms and hands.

All that you have is a gift from God. If you show public appreciation for all of this (as a general attitude as opposed to a onetime thing), then you won't have to write out a public testimonial identifying yourself as a sex addict.

Learn to insert your gratitude into everyday situations and conversations. For example, when you talk about your children, don't say "I'm fortunate." Instead say, "I'm blessed." When you talk about finding a parking space, don't tell people you were lucky, tell them God came through for you. When you narrowly miss some unfortunate injury, don't tell people it was a close call. Tell them God was on your side and had decided to spare you that particular misfortune.

186

You see? Your attitude in life, if you have the right perspective, will illustrate just how much you acknowledge God's gifts. People won't have to know the whole story of you and your struggle with pornography. In fact, your attitude can tell them even more than that story. Your attitude will show them that you attribute everything to your Creator.

People will see the peace you have. People will admire it. People will want to take part in it. And your attitude of gratitude will tell them how.

Giving Back

This is one point that I cannot stress enough. God has given you a gift. Pass it on.

There are so many other men out there who need support. Men who have lost hope in themselves. Men who struggle with just their day-to-day existence. Men who would do anything if someone would just reach out to them and let them know there is a path to freedom.

But watch out. Your efforts, when it concerns helping people quit porn, should always be on men who actually desire to be free... not on convincing men (or women) that freedom is better. There are many people out there who need Christ, but refuse to accept Him. Stay away from them (or at least, completely avoid the subject when you are around them). Pray for their souls from far off. God will eventually turn them in the right direction. But if you meddle in a situation where purity is not appreciated, you become the enemy... and their fight will involve trying to drag you back down again.

If someone denies that pornography is wrong, then your purity is a constant reminder to them that they live in sin. And they will try to destroy your purity. Little by little, piece by piece, they will chip away at the armor you've fitted to yourself.

A recovering alcoholic can reach out and help someone who needs help. He can be there for him when the drunkard makes his way to a meeting. But the recovering alcoholic cannot follow the drunkard to the corner bar. Because there, the drunkard will kill him.

You cannot follow someone into the darkness and pull them out. They must want to come. And when they do, you should always be waiting for them—ready to give help, forgiveness, and hope in any way you can.

In this way, you will always be honoring God... giving thanks in the most perfect form.

Now let's look at our final list. This is the list you should always be able to refer to. A list you should carry with you (mentally or physically) for the rest of your life.

1. You are praying every day.
2. You are confessing your sins to a priest in a reasonable amount of time.
3. You are giving an accountability partner scheduled updates.
4. You are being honest and apologetic with your spouse, without burdening her with details.
5. You have specific responses to specific temptations, you know what they are, and you practice them constantly.
6. You don't think about your response—you just do it.
7. You keep destructive media out of your home and (as much as possible) out of your place of work.
8. You make every act of sex committed to God and your wife, allowing the possibility for children if it is God's will.
9. You cherish your wife and every night ask yourself if you've cherished her as Jesus cherishes His church.
10. You know your triggers and have prepared responses to them.
11. You keep a list of friends to call... and use them as often as necessary.
12. You are always looking for ways to please God more.

13. You glorify God by 'spreading the Word.'
14. You are vigilant against despair, rationalization, substituting, and complacency. You have a planned strategy against every one of these traps.
15. You take failures in stride and do not overlook them, but do not let them cause despair either.
16. You thank God for your purity.

Chapter 14 – Discussion Questions

Discussion Questions for Men's Support / Accountability Groups

This book was written as a self-help guide for men trying to break away from pornography addiction. Since that time, it has been picked up by several Catholic support and accountability groups, who read it together, commenting on the various aspects and using it as discussion starters.

For this reason, I have published the "Out Of The Darkness Workbook." The workbook has all the questions listed below, but with space for someone to write brief answers.

Whether you use the questions/workbook as a way to do a 'moral inventory' of yourself, or you use it as talking points in a support group is up to you, but I wanted to make the questions available in the book itself, as opposed to forcing people to spend the extra money and shipping for a separate book.

The questions are mostly in groups of 3, to make them suitable for men's groups of 5-10 people. In larger groups, it might be necessary to discuss one question at a time—as sharing in larger groups becomes more difficult without a few single men dominating the sharing time.

Chapter 1
Axioms

Women and Beauty

1) Is there a woman in your life that you believe you are able to fully appreciate and admire, in the way God intended?

2) How does pornography interfere with man's proper respect for women?

3) Do you think your lack of respect for women damages your respect for the Virgin Mother Mary?

Sex

1) Growing up, did the adults in your household have a healthy respect for sexuality?

2) Do you think it's possible to have too much reverence for human sexuality?

3) According to Thomas Aquinas, sex is the most powerful human passion. What other passions do you feel you've over-indulged in?

Men

1) Can you think of things, other than sex, that you've been obsessive about?

2) Do you feel you had a good, male role model growing up?

3) Why do you think a male role model is good for girls as well as boys?

4) Are you a role model for other boys/girls? Do you feel you've done a good job?

Chapter 2
Pornography

What is pornography?

1) Do you feel your obsession with pornography has warped your ability to appreciate images that were, at one time, not inappropriate? IE, do you think everything that tempts *you*, tempts men who do *not* have a pornography addiction?

2) Do you think there is a shift in culture, in defining what is acceptable / unacceptable concerning sexual content?

3) Millenials and Gen Xers have a very different attitude on sexuality and openness—do you notice it and do you think the change is for the better or for the worse?

Why is pornography bad?

1) How has your problem with pornography changed your relationship with God?

2) How do you think your relationship with God would improve, if you were able to overcome your problem with pornography?

3) How do you think others perceive your relationship with God?

Victims of pornography

1) Who suffered the most as a cause from your problem with pornography?

2) Do you think your problem with pornography has caused problems with anyone you have never met?

3) What could you do to help the victims of pornography, once you've conquered your addiction?

Chapter 3
Addiction

Addiction

1) Do you believe you are addicted to pornography?

2) Do you think there are people who are addicted to pornography and do not know it?

3) Is pornography addiction different from other addictions, and how?

Experimentation

1) When did you first experiment with pornography?

2) What kind of effect do you think it had on you then?

3) Were you old enough, at that time, to understand the ramifications of your actions?

Misuse / Abuse

1) How quickly did you move from the experimentation stage to the misuse stage, where you used it to self-medicate?

2) Is there something you could have done, at that time, to put a stop to it?

3) Is there anything outside of your own actions that might have stopped it?

Addiction

1) When do you think you entered the addiction stage?

2) How much of it is ritualized? I.E. how much of the activity has been removed from sexuality and become simply a part of your structured day or a way to deal with stress?

3) How hopeful are you, right now, that this can be overcome?

Escalation

1) How far has your addiction escalated?

2) Do you think, if ignored, your addiction will get worse?

3) What are you afraid of happening?

Why Sex Addiction is Different

1) Why would sex addiction escalate into something much different than drug addiction?

2) Have you had problems with anything besides sex and pornography? Drugs? Alcohol? Gambling?

3) Can you find similarities between drug addiction and pornography addiction?

The Catholic Approach to Addiction

1) What specifically about the Catholic Church makes it more able to help addicts than other Christian churches?

2) What does the Catholic Church offer right now to help men with pornography addiction?

3) What Catholic tools have you used so far to fight your addiction?

Chapter 4
Escape

The Side Effects of Purity

Fear

1) How has fear effected your daily life?

Strengthened Relationships

2) How would your life change if you were able to repair your relationships?

Renewed Interest in Love-Making

3) Do you think your wife notices the effects of your addiction in the bedroom?

Closeness to Christ

1) Do you long for a closer relationship to Christ? Do you pray for it?

Peace with Oneself

2) Are you willing to make an effort to end self-loathing and self-pity?

Other Side Effects

3) What other side effects do you think will bloom from overcoming your addiction?

Stages of Purity

Withdraw

1) How are you dealing with (or how do you plan to deal with) the effects of withdraw as you enter into sexual abstinence?

Honeymoon

2) What kinds of activities would glorify God during your honeymoon stage?

The Test

3) What kinds of back-up plans do you have for when you are really tested?

Maintenance

4) How will you maintain your purity and keep from becoming complacent?

Chapter 5
Recognition / Admission

Impurity is a Choice

1) What kinds of choices have you personally made that are making it difficult, if not impossible, to recover?

2) When have you shifted blame to others, and how can you avoid doing it again?

3) When you are ritualizing (when you have started that process that you know will lead to pornography / masturbation) when do you think you've actually made a choice to willingly sin?

Purity is Also a Choice

1) Do you feel, at times, you've lost hope? How can you regain it?

2) What do you think God's role is, in your recovery?

3) What do you think *your* role is in recovery?

Purity is the Only Way Out

1) Can you think of many times when you've procrastinated chastity (as in, "I'll stop looking at these pictures in just a few seconds") and actually followed through?

2) What are your absolute goals, as you go through this program?

3) How will you measure your success as you get closer to your goals?

Chapter 6
Shine the Light

Light Drives Out Darkness

1) How much work did you do to keep your addiction a secret?

2) The younger generation is much more open about pornography use and masturbation. Do you think this development helps or hurts men?

3) Have you told your wife about your addiction? Did she react to it as you expected (OR) What are you afraid her reaction will be?

Using Confession

1) Have you been open about your addiction with a confessor?

2) Did you parish-shop when you went to confession?

3) Do you think you avoided escalation because of confession?

Finding Accountability

1) What plans have you made to find an accountability partner?

2) How will accountability help you in your battle?

3) What are the drawbacks of using a spouse as an accountability partner?

Who Else to Tell

1) What group of people should you NOT tell about your pornography addiction?

2) Have you told anyone that you regret opening up to?

3) Is there anyone you feel needs to know about your addiction that you are afraid to tell and why?

Chapter 7
Change The Habit

Killing the Roots of Pornography Addiction

1) Do you think you've destroyed your ability to appreciate a woman's beauty as God intended?

Controlling Your Eyes

2) Why is the physical act of *looking away* important for your recovery?

Changing Routines and Patterns

3) What routines will you have to change or eliminate to help you overcome your addiction?

Women

1) Are there any women in your life that you see regularly that are a source of temptation?

Television

2) How much control do you have over the television in your household and how will you eliminate it as a source of temptation?

Magazines (and other print)

3) Have you found a way to keep tempting images from being mailed to you? If not, how will you deal with that specific form of temptation?

The Internet

1) What will you do to eliminate your 'alone time' online?

2) What activities on the computer can you eliminate entirely?

3) Are there any activities (like entertainment) that you are making excuses for?

Mobile

1) How much time do you needlessly spend looking at your phone?

Baths / Showers / Hotels

2) Are these a source of temptation for you? How will you deal with them?

Avoiding Temptations

3) What routines can you change to help eliminate unexpected temptations?

Controlling Your Thoughts

4) What planned distractions will you have ready in order to stop thinking about tempting images?

Chapter 8
Change Your Life

Purifying Your Home

1) What kinds of things are the most difficult for you to give up? Why?

2) Are you able to make drastic changes in your home, or is the decision not yours to make? If not, how will you deal with the belongings of other people in the household that cause temptation?

3) Is there anything you are holding onto that you know you should get rid of?

Purifying Your Workplace

1) Most people have less control of their work areas than their homes—how much actual control do you have?

2) What are your plans for dealing with those areas that create problems but which you have no control over?

3) How do the people you work with see you? Are you 'the Christian guy' that they know not to say certain things around... do they respect this or does it encourage them to be all the more offensive?

Purifying Your Sex Life

1) Is your spouse on board with following Catholic teachings concerning sex? If not, how will you work around that without committing sin?

2) Have you ever gone through an abstinence period? Would your spouse be on board with this?

3) If your spouse is unwilling (or if she is unaware of your pornography addiction), what other physical pleasures could you abstain from as a substitute for abstaining from sex?

Setting New Standards

1) What specific changes will you make in your daily life to keep your mind 'out of the gutter?'

2) How do you think these changes will be perceived by friends, family, and coworkers?

3) What will be the most difficult for you to change? How do you plan to change despite this difficulty?

Chapter 9
Break All Triggers

Differentiating Between Triggers and Temptations

1) Do you think you have a good understanding of triggers vs temptations?

2) How could someone 'retrain' their body to turn away from sin?

3) What kinds of triggers are most common for men in today's culture?

Knowing Your Triggers

1) What do you think your most obvious triggers are?

2) Have you completed steps to find less apparent triggers? What are they, or what do you plan to do to uncover them?

3) How far removed from sexuality are your triggers?

Changing Your Responses

1) Which triggers in your life are avoidable?

2) Which triggers in your life can you change by reacting to them differently?

3) What activities can you engage in in order to change your response to specific triggers?

Breaking Behavior Patterns

1) What specific patterns in your life are the most important for you to break?

2) Do you have any people you can call to help you through triggers?

3) What other ways can you find to turn destructive patterns into patterns of virtue?

Chapter 10
Include God

Accepting Forgiveness

1) Do you feel that God has forgiven you?

2) Do you think God has plans for you, despite your weaknesses?

3) Other than pornography, what kinds of things in your life are preventing you from a complete alliance with Jesus Christ?

Overcoming Other Habits and Problems

1) What other habits must you overcome, and how will you overcome them?

2) What specific changes can you make in your daily routines to help you overcome them?

3) Would help from another person make it easier for you to overcome them?

Spending Time with God

1) What time have you set aside each day to talk to God?

2) During times not specifically devoted to God, how often do you think about or talk to God?

3) Does God talk back to you?

Chapter 11
Avoiding Traps

Avoiding Despair

1) As mentioned in Chapter 4, in **The Stages Of Purity**, your purity will be tested by despair. How will you deal with it?

2) How susceptible are you to despair?

3) What kinds of activities can you force yourself to engage in to overcome it?

Avoiding Rationalization

1) How could you stay focused on the truth? Do you have other men you can share with to help weed the lies out of your thinking?

Avoiding Substitutes

2) How likely are you to use a substitute that is just as destructive as pornography? How can you avoid it?

Avoiding Complacency

3) Many men get complacent within a very short time—even weeks after giving up pornography. What boundaries can you create to keep yourself from failing because of complacency?

Chapter 12
Bounce Back From Failure

Reacting to Failure

1) What do you consider to be a failure? List some failures and their levels of importance. I.e., looking at a girl – 3, looking at pornography – 7.

Learning from Failure

2) It's easier to learn from failures when you discuss it with an accountability partner. Do you have one? How else can you find a way to discover *why* you fail?

Bouncing Back

3) What kinds of actions can you take to keep small failures from becoming big ones?

Chapter 13
Thank God

Thanking God Privately

1) What are you thankful for?

Thanking God Publicly

2) What kinds of activities can you engage in to show God your appreciation?

Giving Back

3) How will you help other men who struggle with pornography addiction?

Printed in Great Britain
by Amazon

79167250R00119